Applied OpenStack Design Patterns

Design solutions for production-ready infrastructure with OpenStack components

First Edition

Uchit Vyas

Apress®

Applied OpenStack Design Patterns

Uchit Vyas
Ahmedabad, Gujarat
India

ISBN-13 (pbk): 978-1-4842-2453-3   ISBN-13 (electronic): 978-1-4842-2454-0
DOI 10.1007/978-1-4842-2454-0

Library of Congress Control Number: 2016962448

Managing Director: Welmoed Spahr
Lead Editor: Nikhil Karkal
Technical Reviewer: Bharath Thriuveedula
Editorial Board: Steve Anglin, Pramila Balan, Laura Berendson, Aaron Black, Louise Corrigan, Jonathan Gennick, Robert Hutchinson, Celestin Suresh John, Nikhil Karkal, James Markham, Susan McDermott, Matthew Moodie, Natalie Pao, Gwenan Spearing
Coordinating Editor: Prachi Mehta
Copy Editor: Karen Jameson
Compositor: SPi Global
Indexer: SPi Global
Artist: SPi Global

Distributed to the book trade worldwide by Springer Science+Business Media New York, 233 Spring Street, 6th Floor, New York, NY 10013. Phone 1-800-SPRINGER, fax (201) 348-4505, e-mail orders-ny@springer-sbm.com, or visit www.springeronline.com. Apress Media, LLC is a California LLC and the sole member (owner) is Springer Science + Business Media Finance Inc (SSBM Finance Inc). SSBM Finance Inc is a **Delaware** corporation.

For information on translations, please e-mail rights@apress.com, or visit www.apress.com.

Apress and friends of ED books may be purchased in bulk for academic, corporate, or promotional use. eBook versions and licenses are also available for most titles. For more information, reference our Special Bulk Sales–eBook Licensing web page at www.apress.com/bulk-sales.

Any source code or other supplementary materials referenced by the author in this text are available to readers at www.apress.com. For detailed information about how to locate your book's source code, go to www.apress.com/source-code/. Readers can also access source code at SpringerLink in the Supplementary Material section for each chapter.

Printed on acid-free paper

Contents at a Glance

Contents

About the Author

Uchit Vyas is an IT industry veteran, cloud technologist at heart, and a hands-on Automation/DevOps Architect at ReanCloud. Through his speaking, writing, and analysis, he helps businesses take advantage of the emerging technologies. Uchit loves to play chess and Age of Empires, which helps him to clearly see the impact of ideas, research, and automation-empowering economies of IT.

Uchit works with large IT organizations to automate traditional datacenter flow, explores new-age tools and technologies, and defines solutions and best practices for small and large enterprises with DevOps fundamentals. He has worked at world-class product and service companies like SAP, Infosys, and ReanCloud during which time he analyzed various cloud platforms, Big Data, Infrastructure Automation, Containers, DevOps, and Continuous Delivery.

He has also published various books on Amazon cloud platform and Enterprise Service Bus: *Mule ESB Cookbook*, *AWS Development Essentials*, *Mastering AWS Development*, *DynamoDB Applied Design Patterns*; and he is still working on more books.

About the Technical Reviewer

Bharath Thriuveedula is a software engineer at Imaginea Technologies Inc., and a Core reviewer and key contributor to the OpenStack Tacker, Heat translator projects. He is a contented individual who is passionate about open source technologies and an evangelist who is focused to make his mark in the Cloud/NFV domains. He worked on custom solutions for the NFV Orchestration and his other interests are Containers and Distributed systems.

Acknowledgments

I dedicate this book to my family and friends. A special thanks to my loving parents, Hamendra Vyas and Shreya Vyas, whose words of encouragement and push for tenacity always provided the necessary inspiration. I also dedicate this book to my wife, Riddhi Vyas, who never left my side during the whole writing process and is very special to me.

—Uchit Vyas

Introduction

From the last decade, many IT giants moved their existing infrastructure to OpenStack cloud to get complete controlled and customizable environments. This book is not focused on being a how-to guide or setup book; it is aimed for design solutions only to gain the maximum from OpenStack components. To understand the private cloud infrastructure of OpenStack and its flow, understanding underneath architecture is very important. So in the first part of the book, readers will learn the basics of OpenStack and its component design. With this design understanding, readers can map their application flow and the behavior to start with OpenStack components.

Once the component knowledge and proven architecture design patterns have been set, we will deep dive into OpenStack underneath the behavior to map native infrastructure and application with OpenStack architecture. With this core understanding, we will move toward the component design implementation for native applications on OpenStack to start as a small protocol model. Once the model has been set, users can start to utilize different component implementations of OpenStack with their native application structure. Later in this book, we will define the multi-node compute resource management and clustering solutions to define the High Availability (HA) with OpenStack.

In the later stages of the book, we will focus on resource management and scheduling in OpenStack to map users' requests and allocation. The readers will gain the insight of a resource manager algorithm and native VM provisioning with respect to application components and configuration. In this part, users will learn the common VM provisioning related best practices mapping with respect to resource and capacity management of OpenStack infrastructure.

A little bit later we will focus on design solutions for security implementation and orchestration by including the complete SDLC of the native applications on OpenStack. By understanding security components and its native algorithm, users will be able to design custom profiles for authentication and authorization on OpenStack. With monitoring and metering design, an admin can tweak the resource configurations for specific components and for particular profiles. In the last, but not least part, we will describe the solution patterns for networking components of OpenStack to reduce latency and quick communication gateways between underneath components of OpenStack and native applications. Finally, we will define the end-to-end orchestration with OpenStack by enabling the DevOps/Automation best practices and Orchestration to implement event-based solutions.

CHAPTER 1

■ ■ ■

Designing Your First Cloud with OpenStack

Over the years, the IT infrastructure domain has been moving from traditional ways to IAAS (Infrastructure-as-a-Service). Many giant organizations have implemented IAAS based on the OpenStack Cloud platform to build and run their native applications, including infrastructure components like compute, storage, and networking. Rackspace and NASA are the pioneer contributors for the OpenStack project as NASA contributed their "Nebula" platform for compute resources and Rackspace contributed their "Cloud Files" for Object Storage.

OpenStack's unique features make it a very adoptive and fast-evolving Open Source project, using widely open platform-based integrated solutions, user-friendly dashboards, and flexibility. OpenStack can fit with multiple environment-based applications where "dev" or "test" or "prod" environments exist because of its flexible components and simpler design. The core technologies beyond OpenStack combine internally related projects with various parts including APIs, SDKs, and CLIs for in-house or cloud environmental solutions and management of infrastructure. Moreover, almost all OpenStack APIs are extensible, meaning you can keep compatibility with a core set of calls while giving access to more resources and innovating through API extensions endpoints.

The OpenStack project is a widely adopted and globally collaborative approach for developers and cloud computing technologists. The OpenStack collaborative platform can be used for both public and private clouds.

Perhaps you are working on an app or web-based project and you are going to plan, for example, a vacation. Or for simplicity, let's say you are building some new apartments in your area or redesigning your trendy bungalow. In each of these situations, you will need a mind-blowing strategy. A well-known Japanese military leader, Miyamoto Musashi, wrote the following impressive statement — in *The Book of Five Rings*:

> *In strategy, it is important to see distant things as if they were close and to take a distanced view of close things.*

As of recent times, Cloud and DevOps can be categorized into the following general categories:

- Software as a Service (SaaS)
- Platform as a Service (PaaS)
- Infrastructure as a Service (IaaS)

Electronic supplementary material The online version of this chapter (doi:10.1007/978-1-4842-2454-0_1) contains supplementary material, which is available to authorized users.

© Uchit Vyas 2016
U. Vyas, *Applied OpenStack Design Patterns*, DOI 10.1007/978-1-4842-2454-0_1

Today, the most common issues persisting in the cloud world are to achieve agility, speed, and service uptime up to 100%. All major datacenter solution provider companies are trying to get ready for the future's next-generation datacenter providers. Even in cloud, most of the public cloud vendors have expensive IT systems; however, in the next couple of years, these systems will be out of date.

The major changes for the new-generation datacenter has evolved into the new model approach and adoption for the provisioning and deployment of new software and hardware. To handle the new age of cloud load, modern datacenters have to enable the multi-tenant model for scaling the approach. It is a huge step in datacenter technology to shift their way of handling an entire infrastructure.

The next generation of Automation and DevOps for infrastructure has allowed system administrators and operators to deploy and deliver a fully automated infrastructure within a fraction of the time. The next-generation datacenter and automation will reduce all of the infrastructure components including storage, network, compute, etc., as a single scalable and agile unit. So it's the administrator's responsibility to code the infrastructure as per-environment requirements. To perform and adopt the next-generation cloud mechanism where OpenStack comes as the ringmaster here to support next-generation datacenter Operating System. The ubiquitous influence of OpenStack has been felt by many global giant cloud enterprises like Rackspace, Red Hat, and Cisco, to name but a few. Nowadays most of the cloud services providers are big giants running very large autoscaled private clouds based on OpenStack for their customers and internal units.

Finally, based on what OpenStack can do, why should you use it? Well, OpenStack has very rich community support, enhanced documentation, and elaborate tutorials. Let's jump into the OpenStack design part and its architecture.

Ultimately, the goal of this chapter is to get you from where you are today to the point where you can confidently build a private cloud based on OpenStack with your own design choice.

This chapter will cover the following points:

- Getting familiar with the architecture of OpenStack and the way its different core components co-relate with each other

- Learning how to design an OpenStack environment by choosing the right core services for your environment

- Designing the first OpenStack architecture for a large-scale environment while bearing in mind that OpenStack can be designed in numerous ways

At the conclusion of these first chapters, you will have a solid base of ways to plot your essential functions and infrastructure modules by placing the specifics under the OpenStack lid. You will also understand how OpenStack components work together and be prepared for the next step of our exploration by entreating an OpenStack ecosystem in an intuitive foundation with best practices.

Though the attractive part of OpenStack might be to construct your own cloud, there are numerous ways to achieve this purpose. Possibly the meekest of each is an appliance-style clarification. You grip an appliance, unload it, plug in the power and the network, and watch it transmute into an OpenStack cloud with nominal further configuration. Rarely, if any, other open source cloud commodities have such turnkey possibilities. If a turnkey resolution is fascinating to you, take a glance at Nebula cloud.

Nevertheless, hardware selection is crucial for various applications, so if this pertains to you, know that there are some software allocations presented that you can ride on servers, storage, and network commodities of your choosing. Recognized giants named Red Hat and SUSE offer enterprise OpenStack explanations and support.

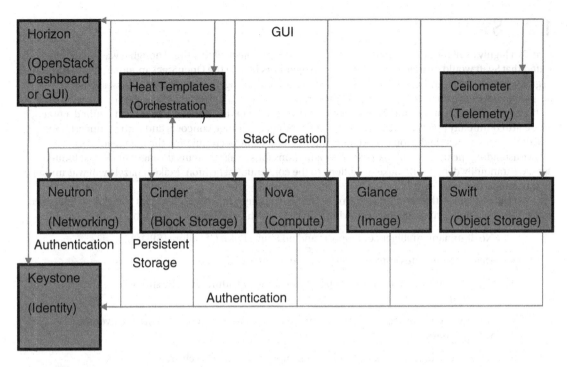

Figure 1-1. *OpenStack request workflow*

To object, deploy, and configure OpenStack, architects must recognize the rational design. Before jumping into the architecture of OpenStack, we need to refresh the basic concepts and usage of each core module. In order to get a clear understanding of how it plants, it will be applicable to first sketchily parse the building chunks that mark its grind.

Supposing that you have previously mounted OpenStack or even positioned it in a small or medium-sized ecosystem, let's place the fundamental modules under the lid of OpenStack podium and go a little more advanced by taking the use cases and asking the following: what is the tenacity of such a component?

1.1 Keystone

From an architectural viewpoint, Keystone offerings are the easiest type of service in the OpenStack alignment. It is the primary module that stipulates identity tune-up, and it assimilates meanings for authentication, catalog services, and policies to register and accomplish different tenants and users in the OpenStack endeavors. The API requests concerning OpenStack services are being managed by Keystone to confirm that the right user or service is able to exploit the entreated OpenStack service. Keystone achieves plentiful validation apparatuses such as username/password as well as a token authentication-based system. Moreover, it is possible to incorporate it with an accessible back-end directory such as Lightweight Directory Access Protocol (LDAP) and the Pluggable Authentication Module (PAM).

A comparable real-life paradigm is a city resolute. You can grip a travel card and turnover by traveling a definite number of places during a certain period of time. Before you start traveling, you have to test for the card to gain entrance to the city at the main gates of the city domiciles. All the times that you would like to attempt a new place for a visit, you must check in at the place gate machine. This will produce a request, which is diagrammed to a central authentication system to pattern the validity of the card and its permit, to profit the entreated place. By comparison, the token in Keystone can be competed to the travel card excluding that it does not ebb anything from your request. The identity service is being measured as a dominant and communal authentication system that feeds access to the consumers.

1.2   Swift

Swift is a highly available, distributed, eventually consistent object/blob store. Though it was succinctly stated that Swift would be made obtainable to the operators beside the OpenStack modules, it is fascinating to grasp how Swift has endowed what is signified to be cloud storage. Most of the businesses in the last period did not fleece their doubts almost at precarious part of the IT groundwork — the storage where the statistics are alleged. Thus, obtaining exclusive hardware to be in the innocuous zone had befitted a practice. There are continually assured encounters that are handled by storage concocts and with no uncertainty, one of these tests include the job of curtailing interruption while accumulating the data readiness. Notwithstanding the upswing of many keen explanations for storage systems throughout the last limited ages, we tranquilly demand to make deviations to the conventional fashion. Make it hazy! Swift was initiated to accomplish this task.

We will consensus the givens distressing to the Swift strategy for subsequent, but you should endure in communication that Swift is an object stowing software, which has a number of notable points:

- No dominant intelligence signposts and no Single Point Of Failure (SPOF)

- Healing designates auto-recovery in circumstance of disaster

- Particularly ascendable for hefty petabytes store and admittance by surpassing matching

- Improved enactment, which is accomplished by dissemination of the freight over the storage nodes

- Reasonable hardware can be utilized for superfluous storage clusters

1.3   Glance

The employment of Glance is to be an image registry. Starting here, we can accomplish how OpenStack has secured the best approach to being further segmental and approximately coupled key component standards. Utilizing Glance to heap virtual disk pictures is a choice. From a compositional level, joining added dynamic approaches to a demand image report by means of the image storage Programming interface offered by Look over a self-overseeing image storage back end, for example, Quick conveys further refreshing working and taught framework hidden luxuries. With this strategy, a client will be savvy to record another virtual disk image, on occasion, to stream it from an amazingly available and surplus store. On this adjusted stride, as a specialized mechanic, you may give the appearance of another test execution.

1.4   Cinder

Truly, the administration of the persistent block storage can be incorporated into OpenStack by exercising Cinder. Its key competence to extant block-level storage delivers raw volumes that can be assembled into logical volumes in the filesystem and attached in the virtual machine (VM).

Certain landscapes that Cinder deals with are as follows:

- Volume supervision: this admits the making or removal of a volume

- Snapshot administration: this consents the design or erasure of a snapshot of volumes

- You can attach or detach volumes from VMs

- You can replicate volumes

- Volume construction from snapshots is achievable via Cinder

- You can duplicate images to volumes and vice versa

Numerous storage selections have been projected in the OpenStack fundamentals. Deprived of hesitation, you may be questioning this: what kind of storage will be paramount for you? With a policymaking technique, an evaluation of pros and cons must be completed. Table 1-1 is a very naive table that designates the transformation among the storage types in OpenStack to evade any misperception when picking the storage administration decision for your forthcoming project:

Table 1-1. *Storage Comparison*

Measurement	Storage Category	
	Object storage	Block storage
Functioning	-	OK
Database storage	-	OK
Reinstating backup data	OK	OK
Setup for volume sources	-	OK
Persistence	OK	OK
Admission	Wherever	Inside VM
Image storage	OK	-

It is equally important to note that dissimilar Glance and Keystone facilities, Cinder landscapes are conveyed by coordinating volume providers concluded the configurable operation driver's designs such as IBM, NetApp, Nexenta, and VMware.

If Cinder is proven to be an ideal solution or a replacement of the old nova-volume service that existed before the Folsom release on an architectural level, it is important to know that Cinder has organized and created a catalog of block-based storage devices with several differing characteristics. However, this is obvious if we consider the limitation of commodity storage redundancy and autoscaling. Eventually, the block storage service as the main core of OpenStack can be improved if a few gaps are filled, such as the addition of these values:

- Quality of service

- Replication

- Tiering

The previously stated Cinder particular uncovers its non-seller lock-in trademark, where it is conceivable to change the back end effortlessly or perform information relocation between two distinctive storage back ends. In this manner, a superior storage outline design in a Cinder use case will bring an outsider into the amusement of versatility.

1.5 Nova

As you may already know, Nova is the most unique center part of OpenStack. From an engineering level, it is viewed as a standout among the most confusing parts of OpenStack.

More or less, Nova runs continuously, which works together to react to a client demand into running VM. How about we separate the blob image of Nova by accepting that its engineering as a disseminated application needs organization so that assignments can be done between various segments?

1.5.1   nova-api

The nova-API segment acknowledges and reacts to the end client and figures the Programming interface calls. The end clients or different parts speak with the OpenStack Nova Programming interface to make cases by means of OpenStack Programming interface or EC2 Programming interface.

1.5.2   nova-compute

The nova-compute process part is basically a laborer daemon that makes and ends VM occurrences by means of the hypervisor's APIs (XenAPI for XenServer, Libvirt KVM, and the VMware Programming interface for VMware).

1.5.3   nova-volume

The nova-volume part deals with the creation, joining, and separating of N volumes to process occurrences (like Amazon's EBS).

1.5.4   nova-network

The nova-network part acknowledges organizing undertakings from the Queue and after that plays out these assignments to control the system, (for example, setting up connecting interfaces or changing the IP table principles).

1.5.5   nova-scheduler

The nova-scheduler part takes a VM case's solicitation from the line and figures out where it ought to run (particularly which process server hosts it should keep running on). At an application engineering level, the term planning or scheduler summons an orderly way to hunt down the best outfit for an offered framework to enhance its execution.

Nova additionally gives console benefits that permit end clients to get to the console of the virtual case through an intermediary: for example, nova-console, nova-novncproxy, and nova-consoleauth.

By zooming out the general parts of OpenStack, we find that Nova communicates with a few services: for example, Cornerstone for confirmation, Look for images, and Horizon for the web interface. For instance, the Glance connection is focal; the Programming interface procedure can transfer any question to Look, while nova-compute will download images to dispatch images.

1.6   Queue

Queue gives a focal center point to pass messages between daemons. This is the place data is shared between various Nova daemons by encouraging the correspondence between discrete procedures in a non-concurrent way.

Any service can, without much of a stretch, speak with some other service by means of the API's service. One noteworthy position of the queuing framework is that it can cushion an extensive support workload. As opposed to utilizing a RPC service, a queue framework can queue an extensive workload and give an inevitable consistency.

1.7   Database

A database stores the greater part of the fabrication time and runtime state for the cloud foundation, including example sorts that are accessible for use, occasions being used, accessible systems, and activities. It is the second crucial bit of sharing data in all OpenStack parts.

1.8   Neutron

Neutron gives a genuine Network as a Service (NaaS) between interface gadgets that are overseen by OpenStack administrations, for example, Nova. There are different attributes that should be considered for Neutron:

- It permits clients to make their own particular systems and afterward join server interfaces to them.

- Its pluggable back-end design gives clients a chance to exploit the item rigging or merchant upheld gear.

- Extensions permit extra system services, programming, or equipment to be coordinated.

Neutron has numerous center system features and includes ones that are continually developing. Some of these components are helpful for switches, virtual switches, and the SDN organizing controllers. Neutron presents new ideas, which incorporate the following:

- Port: Ports in Neutron allude to the virtual switch associations. These associations are the place cases and system services joined to systems. At the point when joined to the subnets, the characterized Mac and IP locations of the interfaces are connected to them.

- Networks: Neutron characterizes systems as disengaged Layer 2 system sections. Administrators will consider systems to be coherent switches that are executed by the Linux spanning apparatuses, Open vSwitch, or some other programming. Not at all like physical systems, this can be characterized by either the administrators or clients in OpenStack.

- Routers: Routers give entryways between different Networks.

- Private and gliding IPs: Private and drifting IP addresses allude to the IP deliveries that are appointed to occasions. Private IP locations are obvious inside the occurrence and are typically a part of a private system devoted to an occupant. This system permits the inhabitant's examples to impart when separated from alternate occupants.

In Neutron's low-level coordination of Layer 1 through Layer 3 parts, for example, IP tending to, subnetting, and directing can likewise oversee abnormal state services. For instance, Neutron gives Load Balancing as a Service(LBaaS) using HAProxy to circulate the movement among different process node instances.

1.9   Horizon

Horizon is the web dashboard that pools all the diverse sorts out from your OpenStack biological system.

Horizon gives a web front end to OpenStack administrations. As of now, it incorporates all the OpenStack administrations and, in addition, some brooded ventures. It was composed as a stateless and informationless web application — it simply does starting activities in the OpenStack services by means of Programming interface calls and showing data that OpenStack comes back to the Horizon. It doesn't keep any information aside from the session data in its own information store. It is intended to be a reference usage that can be altered and stretched out by administrators for a specific cloud. It shapes the premise for a few open mists — most remarkably the HP Open Cloud; and at its heart is its extensible particular way to deal with development.

Horizon depends on a progression of modules called boards that characterize the cooperation of every administration. Its modules can be empowered or incapacitated, contingent upon the service accessibility of the specific cloud. Notwithstanding this practical adaptability, Horizon is anything but difficult to style with Falling Templates (CSS).

Most cloud supplier appropriations give an organization's particular topic to their dashboard usage.

1.10   Shared File Systems

Shared File Frameworks administration gives an arrangement of administrations to administration of shared File frameworks in a multi-inhabitant cloud environment. The services look like OpenStack block-based storage administration from the OpenStack Block Storage administration venture. With the Shared File Frameworks service, you can make a remote record framework, mount the record framework on your cases, and afterward read and compose information from your examples to and from your document framework.

The Shared File Frameworks administration fills the same need as the Amazon Elastic File System Framework (EFS) does.

The OpenStack File Share administration permits you to offer shared document frameworks administration to OpenStack clients in your establishment. The Shared File Frameworks administration can keep running in a solitary hub or various node design. The Common Record Frameworks administration can be arranged to procurement offers from one or more back closures, so it is required to announce no less than one back end. Shared File Framework administration contains a few configurable segments.

It is vital to comprehend these parts:

- Share systems

- Shares

- Multi-occupancy

- Back closes

The Shared Record Frameworks administration comprises four sorts of services, a large portion of which are like those of the block storage administration:

- manila-programming interface (API)

- manila-information

- manila-scheduler

- manila-share

Establishment of the initial three - manila-programming interface, manila-information, and manila-scheduler are normal for all organizations. Be that as it may, arrangement of manila-share is back-end particular and can contrast from organization to sending.

1.11   Telemetry

Indeed, even in the cloud business, suppliers must utilize a multistep process for charging. The obliged ventures to charge for use in a cloud domain are metering, rating, and charging. Since the supplier's necessities might be excessively particular for a mutual arrangement, rating and charging arrangements can't be planned in a typical module that fulfills all. Furnishing clients with estimations on cloud administrations is required to meet the deliberate administration meaning of distributed computing.

The Telemetry administration was initially intended to bolster charging frameworks for OpenStack cloud assets. This anticipation just covers the metering part of the required preparation for charging. This administration gathers data about the framework and stores it as tests with a specific end goal to give information about anything that can be charged. Notwithstanding framework estimations, the Telemetry benefit additionally catches occasional warnings activated when different activities are executed in the OpenStack framework. This information is caught as occasions and puts away close-by metering information.

The rundown of meters is ceaselessly developing, which makes it conceivable to utilize the information gathered by Telemetry for various purposes, other than charging. For instance, the autoscaling highlight in the Orchestration administration can be activated by alerts that this module sets and afterward gets advised inside Telemetry.

1.12   Bare Metal

The Bare Metal administration gives physical equipment rather than virtual machines. It likewise gives a few reference drivers, which influence regular innovations like PXE and IPMI, to cover an extensive variety of equipment. The pluggable driver engineering additionally permits merchant particular drivers to be included for enhanced execution or usefulness not given by reference drivers. The Bare Metal administration makes physical servers as simple to procurement as virtual machines in a cloud, which thus will open up new roads for ventures and administration suppliers.

1.13   Orchestration

Orchestration is an arrangement motor that gives the likelihood of dispatching various composite cloud applications in light of formats as content documents that can be dealt with like code. A local Heat Orchestration template (HOT) configuration is developing; however it additionally tries to furnish similarity with the AWS CloudFormation layout group, so that numerous current CloudFormation formats can be propelled on OpenStack.

The OpenStack Organization benefit, an apparatus for coordinating mists, naturally arranges and sends assets in stacks. The arrangements can be basic, for example: conveying WordPress on Ubuntu with a SQL back end; or mind boggling, such as beginning a server gathering that autoscales by beginning and halting utilizing continuous CPU stacking data from the Telemetry administration.

Organization stacks are characterized with formats, which are nonprocedural reports. Layouts portray errands regarding assets, parameters, inputs, requirements, and conditions. At the point when the Organization administration was initially presented, it worked with AWS CloudFormation layouts, which are in the JSON group.

The Orchestration benefit likewise runs Heat Layout formats that are composed in YAML. YAML is a pithy documentation that freely takes after basic traditions (colons, returns, spaces) that are like Python or Ruby. In this way, it is simpler to compose, parse, grep, produce with apparatuses, and keep up source-code administration frameworks.

Coordination can be given through CLI and RESTful inquiries. The arrangement administration gives both an OpenStack-local REST Programming interface and a CloudFormation-good Question Programming interface. The coordination administration is additionally incorporated with the OpenStack dashboard to perform stack capacities through a web interface.

1.14   A Sample Architecture Setup

Fundamentally, what you ought to consider in any case is the obligation in the Cloud. Contingent upon your distributed computing mission, it is key to comprehend what a planning IaaS is. The accompanying are the utilization cases:

- Cloud administration financier: This is an encouraging delegate part of Cloud administration utilizations for a few suppliers, including upkeep

- Cloud administration supplier: This gives XaaS to private cases

- Self-cloud benefit: This gives XaaS its own IT for private utilization

Aside from the learning of the previously stated cloud service model suppliers, there are a couple of expert keys that you ought to consider with a specific end goal to convey all-around characterized engineering to a decent premise that is prepared to be sent.

In spite of the fact that the framework engineering plan has advanced and is joined by the selection of a few procedure systems, numerous undertakings have effectively sent OpenStack situations by experiencing a 3D procedure — an applied model configuration, intelligent model outline, and physical model configuration.

It may be clear that many-sided quality increments from the calculated to the consistent outline and from the coherent to the physical configuration.

1.14.1   The Conceptual Model Design

As the primary applied stage, we will have an abnormal state reflection on what we will require from certain nonspecific classes from the OpenStack engineering:

Class	Role
Compute	Stores virtual machine images Provides a user interface
Image	Stores disk files Provides a user interface
Object storage	Provides a user interface
Block storage	Provides volumes Provides a user interface
Network	Provides network connectivity Provides a user interface
Identity	Provides authentication
Dashboard	Graphical user interface
Orchestration	Provides orchestration for various components
Telemetry	Provides metering service

1.14.2   The Logical Model Design

In light of the applied reflection stage, we are prepared to build the sensible outline. Most likely, you have smart ideas about various OpenStack center parts, which will be the premise of the detailing of the consistent configuration that is finished by setting out their intelligent representations. Despite the fact that we have effectively taken the center of the OpenStack administrations segment by segment, you may need to create an outline of them to a sensible arrangement inside the complete configuration.

To do as such, we will begin by laying out the relations and conditions between the services center of OpenStack. Above all, we intend to dig into the building level by keeping the subtle elements for the end. Accordingly, we will consider the repartition of the OpenStack administrations between the new bundle benefits — the cloud controller and the compute node. You may ask why such an idea experiences a physical configuration order. Notwithstanding, seeing the cloud controller and compute nodes as straightforward bundles that typify a group of OpenStack services, this will help you refine your outline at an early stage. Besides, this methodology will arrange ahead of time further high accessibility and adaptability highlights, which permit you to present them later in more detail.

Accordingly, the physical model outline will be explained taking into account the past hypothetical stages by allocating parameters and qualities to our configuration.

Clearly, in an exceptionally accessible setup, we ought to accomplish a level of repetition in every administration inside OpenStack. You may wonder about the basic OpenStack administrations asserted in the initial segment of this part — the database and message line. Why wouldn't they be able to be independently grouped or bundled all alone? This is an applicable inquiry. Keep in mind that we are still in the second intelligent stage where we attempt to plunge gradually and softly into the foundation without diving into the points of interest. In addition, we continue going from general to particular models, where we concentrate more on the nonspecific subtle elements. Decoupling RabbitMQ or MySQL starting now and into the foreseeable future may prompt your outline being ignored. Then again, you may chance skipping other nonexclusive outline points. Then again, setting up a nonspecific legitimate configuration will help you to not stick to only one conceivable blend, but subsequent to the future, physical outlines will depend on it.

Compute nodes are moderately basic as they are expected just to run the virtual machine's workload. Keeping in mind the end goal to deal with the VMs, the nova-register administration can be doled out for each process hub. Additionally, we ought not to overlook that the process nodes won't be separated; a Neutron operator and a discretionary Ceilometer figure specialist may run this node.

1.14.3 Storage Layout

By now you should have a more profound comprehension of the capacity sorts inside OpenStack—Swift and Cinder.

Be that as it may, we didn't cover an outsider programming characterized capacity called Ceph, which may consolidate or supplant either or both of Swift and Cinder.

Eventually, a storage framework turns out to be more confounded when it confronts an exponential development in the measure of information. Along these lines, the outlining of your storage framework is one of the basic strides that is required for a hearty design.

Contingent upon your OpenStack business size environment, what amount of information do you have to store? Will your future PaaS develop an extensive variety of utilizations that run substantial investigation information? Shouldn't something be said about the arranged Environment as a Service (EaaS) model? Engineers should incrementally move down their virtual machine's snapshots. We require steady storage.

Try not to tie up all of your investments in one place. This is the reason we will incorporate Cinder and Swift in the mission. Numerous scholars will ask the accompanying question: in the event that one can be fulfilled by transient storage, why offer block storage? To answer this question, you may consider vaporous capacity as the spot where the end client won't have the capacity to get to the virtual disk connected with its VM when it is ended. Fleeting capacity ought to essentially be utilized as a part of generation that happens in a high-scale environment, where clients are effectively worried about their information, VM, or application. In the event that you arrange that your storage configuration ought to be 100 percent steady, going down everything astutely will improve how you feel. This helps you make sense of the most ideal approach to store information that becomes exponential by utilizing particular systems that permit them to be set aside a few minutes. Keep in mind that the present configuration applies for medium to extensive foundations. Fleeting capacity can likewise be a decision for specific clients, for instance, when they think about working as a test domain. Considering the same case for Swift, we have asserted beforehand that the object storage may be utilized to store machine images, yet when is this the case?

This is the case when you give the additional equipment that satisfies certain Swift prerequisites: replication and repetition. Running a wide creation environment, while putting away machine images on the nearby document framework, is not a good practice. To start with, the image can be gotten to by various administrations and asked for by a large number of clients at once. No big surprise the controller is now depleted by the sending and steering of the solicitations between the diverse APIs notwithstanding the calculation of every asset through disk I/O, memory, and CPU. Every solicitation will bring about execution debasement, yet it won't fall flat! Keeping an image in a filesystem under an overwhelming burden will absolutely convey the controller to a high inertness, and it might fizzle.

Consequently, we should think about inexactly coupled models, where the capacity with a particular execution is viewed as a best fit for the creation environment.

1.14.4   Networking

A standout among the most entangled framework outlining steps is the part concerning the system! Presently, we should look in the engine to perceive how all the diverse administrations that were characterized already should be associated.

1.14.4.1   The logical networking design

OpenStack demonstrates an extensive variety of networking administration designs that shift between the fundamental and muddled. Terms, for example, Open vSwitch, Neutron combined with the VLAN division, and VMware NSX with Neutron are not naturally evident from their appearance to have the capacity to be executed without getting their utilization case in our configuration. In this way, this essential stride suggests that you may vary between various system topologies as a result of the explanations for why each decision was made and why it might work for a given use case.

OpenStack has moved from shortsighted network components to muddled elements; obviously there is a reason — more adaptability! This is the reason OpenStack is here. It brings as much adaptability as it can! It does so without taking any irregular system-related choices.

1.14.4.2   The management network

An orchestrator hub was not depicted already since it is not a local OpenStack service. Distinctive nodes need to get IP addresses, the DNS, and the DHCP administration where the orchestrator node becomes possibly the most important factor. You should likewise remember that in an extensive situation, you will require a node provisioning strategy that your nodes will be designed to boot, by utilizing PXE and TFTP.

1.14.5   The Physical Model Design

At last, we will breathe life into our coherent outline as a physical configuration. At this stage, we have to assign parameters. The physical configuration walls in all the segments that we managed beforehand in the intelligent outline. Obviously, you will acknowledge how such an acceleration in the outline separates the unpredictability of the OpenStack environment and helps us recognize the sorts of equipment details that you will require.

We can begin with a set number of servers just to set the main arrangement of our surroundings adequately. To begin with, we will consider a little production environment that is exceedingly adaptable and extensible. This is the thing that we have secured already — expecting a sudden development and being prepared for an exponentially expanding number of solicitations to service instances.

You need to consider the way that the equipment item determination will fulfill the mission of our gigantic adaptable design.

1.14.5.1   Estimating your hardware capabilities

Since the engineering is being intended to scale on a level plane, a product with financially savvy equipment can be utilized. To expect our framework economy, it is necessary to make some fundamental equipment counts for the principal estimation of what will be needed.

Thinking about the possibility of encountering disputes for assets, for example, CPU, RAM, Network, and disk, you can't sit tight for a specific physical part to come up short before you make a restorative move, which may be more entangled.

How about we examine a genuine case of the effect of thinking a little about scope planning? A Cloud-facilitating organization set up two medium servers: one for an email server, and the other to have as the official site. The organization, which is one of your few customers, developed in a couple of months and in the end, you came up short on circle space. You anticipated that such an issue would be determined in a couple of hours; however it took days. The issue was that every one of the gatherings did not make legitimate utilization of the "cloud," which focuses to the "on interest" way. The email server, which is a standout among the most basic parts of an organization, had been overburdened and the Mean Time To Repair (MTTR) was expanding exponentially. The Cloud supplier did not expect this!

All things considered, it may be strange to record your SLA report and portray in your episode administration area the reason — you didn't expect such a development! Later, subsequent to redeploying the virtual machine with more disk space, the email server would aggravate everybody in the organization with a message saying, "We can validate however our messages are not being sent! They are lined!" The other person could assert, "At long last, I have sent an email and 2 hours later I got a telephone call that is was received." Tragically, the cloud worldview was intended to maintain a strategic distance from such situations and bring more achievement variables that can be accomplished by facilitating suppliers. Limited administration is viewed as an everyday obligation where you need to stay redesigned with respect to programming or equipment updates.

Through a persistent checking procedure of service utilization, you will have the capacity to decrease the IT hazard and give a fast reaction time to the client's needs.

From your first equipment sending, continue running your ability administration forms by circling through tuning, checking, and investigation.

The following stop will consider your tuned parameters and present inside your equipment/programming the right change, which includes a cooperative energy of the change administration process.

We should make our first computation taking into account certain necessities. We mean to run 200 VMs in our OpenStack surroundings.

1.14.5.1.1   CPU calculations

The accompanying is the computation-related presumptions:

- 200 virtual machines
- No CPU oversubscribing Note

Processor oversubscription is characterized as the aggregate number of CPUs that are allocated to all the controlled on virtual machines increased by the equipment CPU cores. On the off chance that this number is larger than the GHz bought, the environment is said to be oversubscribed.

- Total of GHz per core: 2.6 GHz
- Hyper-threading maintained: use factor 2
- Total of GHz per VM (AVG compute units) = 2 GHz
- Total of GHz per VM (MAX compute units) = 16 GHz

- Intel Xeon E5-2648L v2 core CPU = 10

- CPU sockets each server = 2

- Number of CPU cores per VM:

- 16 / (2.6 * 2) = 3.076

- We expect to appoint at least 3 CPU cores per VM

- The recipe for its deviousness will be as tails: max GHz /(total of GHz per core x 1.3 for hyper-threading)

On the off chance that your CPU does not bolster hyper-threading, you should increase the quantity of GHz per center by 1.3 components rather than 2.

Total number of CPU cores:

(200 * 2) / 2.6 = 153.846

We have 153 CPU cores for 200 VMs.

The formula for calculation will be:

(number of VMs x number of GHz per VM) / number of GHz per core

Numeral of core CPU sockets:

153 / 10 = 15.3

We will essentially need 15 sockets.

The formula for calculation will be as follows:

Total amount of sockets / number of sockets per server

Number of socket servers:

15 / 2 = 7.5

You will require around 7 to 8 dual socket servers.

The principle for design will be as follows:

Total number of sockets / Number of sockets per server

The number of VM per server with 8 dual socket servers will be calculated as follows:

200 / 8 = 25

The formula for calculation will be as surveys:

Number of VMs / number of servers

We can deploy 25 VM per server.

1.14.5.1.2   Memory calculations

Based on the previous example, 25 VMs can be deployed per compute node. Memory sizing is also important to avoid making unreasonable resource allocations.

Let's make a list of assumptions:

- 2 GB RAM per VM

- 8 GB RAM maximum vigorous allotment per VM

- Compute nodes accompanying slots of: 2, 4, 8, and 16 GB sticks

- Remember that it alters your financial plan and wishes

- RAM presented per compute node:

- 8 * 25 = 200 GB

- Bearing in mind the number of sticks sustained by the server, you will demand throughout 256 GB installed. Consequently, the total number of RAM sticks mounted can be gauged in the resulting way:

- 256 / 16 = 16

- The procedure for deviousness is as charted

- Total open RAM / MAX Presented RAM-Stick size

1.14.5.2   The network calculations

To satisfy the arrangements that were drawn for the system beforehand, we have to accomplish the best execution and networking administration experience. Here are our assumptions:

- 200 Mbits/second is essential per VM

- Tiniest network latency

To do this, it may be conceivable to serve our VMs by utilizing a 10 GB link for every server, which will give:

```
10000 Mbits/second / 25VMs = 400 Mbits/second
```

This is an extremely fulfilling system. We have to consider another component — a very accessible network design. Along these lines, an option would be utilizing two data switches with at least 24 ports for information. Thinking about growth from now on, two 48-port switches will be in place.

Shouldn't something be said about the development of the rack size? For this situation, you should consider the case of a switch total that uses the Virtual Link Trunking (VLT) innovation between the switches in the accumulation. This element resources every server rack to isolate their connections between the pair of changes to accomplish an intense active-active connections while utilizing the full data transmission ability with no prerequisites for a spreading over spanning tree.

VLT is a Layer 2 link accumulation convention between the servers that are associated with the switches, offering an excess, load-adjusting association with the networking and supplanting the traversing tree convention.

1.14.5.3 Storage calculations

Considering the past illustration, you have to anticipate an underlying storage limit for each server that will serve 25 VMs each. How about we make the accompanying suppositions:

- The utilization of transient stockpiling for a nearby drive for the VM

- 100 GB for capacity for each VM's drive

- The utilization of determined storage for remote connecting volumes to VMs

Credible arithmetic individuals used to indicate for 100 VMs a space of 100*100 = 10 TB of nearby storage.

You can dispense 250 GB of diligent storage for each VM to have 200*200 = 40 TB of tenacious storage.

Subsequently, you can settle the amount of capacity there should be there on the server for helping 20 VMs 150*25 = 3.5 TB of capacity on each of the VM. In the event that you plan to incorporate object storage as we said before, we can accept that we will require 25 TB of object storage.

Most presumably, you have a thought regarding the replication of object storage in OpenStack, which infers the utilization of three times the required space for replication. At the end of the day, you should consider that the arranging of X TB for object storage will be increased by three, consequently taking into account our presumption: 25*3 = 75 TB.

Additionally, on the off chance that you consider an item storage in view of zoning, you will need to commit no less than five times the required space. This implies: 25 * 5 = 125 TB.

Other reflections, such as the greatest storage functioning exploiting SSD, can be beneficial for an improved throughput wherever you can advance further packages to get an improved IOPS. For instance, operational with SSD with 20K IOPS installed in a server with eight slot drives will get this:

(20K * 8) / 25 = 6.4 K Read IOPS and 3.2K Write IOPS

That is not bad for an assembly starter for production environments!

What about best exercises? Is it just a principle? Does anybody observe such principles? Well, let's observe several fine observations underneath the microscope by uncovering the OpenStack approach flavor. In a classic OpenStack production ecosystem, the slightest necessity for disk space per compute node is 300 GB with a minimum RAM of 128 GB and a dual 8-core CPUs.

Let's conceive a development where, due to reasonable restraints, you surprise your first compute node with precious hardware that has a 600 GB disk space, 16-core CPUs, and 256 GB of RAM.

To gain a superior OpenStack atmosphere, you may choose to obtain more hardware — a big one at farfetched prices! A second compute illustration is positioned to scale up.

After this, you may catch on that the requirement is cumulative. You may have a burning desire for diverse compute knobs but keep on enduring scaling up with the hardware. At a certain contact, you will be warned to accomplish your economical limit! There are definitely periods while the paramount exercises aren't in datum the best for your proposal.

If the minimal hardware requirement is strictly followed, it may result in an exponential charge with respect to the hardware overheads, particularly for new development starters. Therefore, you may select what closely plants for you and consider the restraints that exist in your ecosystem. Keep in mind that the paramount pertains are a recommendation; pertain them when you catch what you essential to be deployed and how it would be fixed up.

On the other role, do not switch to principles, but penetrate to procedures. Trades and appeals in the compute node may grow immensely in a short time to a point that a definite big compute node with 16 core CPUs twitches dwindling presentation knowledgeable, while a few tiny compute nodes with 4 core CPUs can advance to wide-ranging the job productively.

1.15 Summary

In this chapter, you learned about the plan features of OpenStack and the essential modules of such an environment. We have also weighed the object deliberations throughout OpenStack and examined the diverse potentials of encompassing its functionalities. Now, we have decent preparation for driving further brewed developments into invention. You may observe that your first fundamental strategy covers most of the serious topics that one can experience through the production deployment and build. In addition, it is vital to note that this first episode might be measured as a key guideline for the next parts of this manuscript. The next sections will delight each notion and technology solution cited in this section in more aspect by enlarging the first essential design. Thus, the next interval will take you from this nonspecific design indication theory to a realistic stage. Fundamentally, you will discover how to organize and inflate what was considered by embracing a competent infrastructure positioning attitude — the DevOps style.

CHAPTER 2

■ ■ ■

Reference Architecture

To appreciate the possible segments that OpenStack offers, it's best to look at essential models that have been demonstrated attempted over live situations based on production design and failover scenarios. So let's begin with two such cases with fundamental turns on the base OS structure (Ubuntu and Red Hat Enterprise Linux) and the Networking platform. There are always contrasts between these two outlines; however, you should find the considerations settled on for the choices in each and, also, a technique for thinking about why it worked well in a given setup.

Since OpenStack is effortlessly configurable and looks easily maintainable according to the given guidelines, with an extensive variety of back-end segments and network outline decisions, it is difficult to create a section that covers all relative OpenStack arrangements in a solitary shot. In this part, I describe outline models to unravel the endeavor of composing the capacities of OpenStack that can exist in a real production environment or the mathematics that can be useful to estimate your resources for OpenStack.

2.1 Operational Contemplations

It's natural that various operational parts will be impacted all-around valuable cloud platform arrangement decisions. In a vast production-ready setup, it is not possible for admin members to be able to keep up with cloud platform constantly with any automation technique and self-healing scripts. This differs from the administrative engineer's perspective that he is accountable for building or configuring the establishment of a cloud platform. It is basic to fuse the production operations limit in the masterminding and plan wipes out of the all-time up production-based platform setup.

Moreover, consider the SLAs that are lawfully restricting duties that offer certifications to manage availability and uptime of the cloud platform. SLAs describe levels of openness and uptime that drive the specific blueprint, every now and again with risk charges for not meeting the SLA-based duties. The strictness of the SLA deals with the level of excess and adaptability in the OpenStack cloud framework platform. Knowing when and where to set up, which components need to be set up and actualized, and HA are affected by rules set by the SLA. A part of the SLA expressions that will impact the layout include the following:

- Ensures API availability and uptime propose various organizational administrations clubbed with HA-based LBs and other components.

- Complete Platform uptime protections will impact the switch arrange and may require loose coupling of components, routing, and electricity/cooling supply.

- Platform security methodologies requirements should be considered into platform configurations and production deployments.

© Uchit Vyas 2016
U. Vyas, *Applied OpenStack Design Patterns*, DOI 10.1007/978-1-4842-2454-0_2

2.1.1   Backing Up and Practicality

OpenStack platform needs administrative architects to learn and acknowledge setup outline components. The level of capacities for the storage and the level of segments of the operations and designing members are dependent on the size and inspiration driving the OpenStack cloud platform setup. A gigantic cloud platform management supplier or a telecom supplier will likely be managed by a specially arranged, proven operations affiliation. A more diminutive setup will most likely rely on upon a smaller combined staff that has to incorporate advancement and operations, as well as handling the solidified design, layout, and operations limits of the OpenStack parts and complete platform.

Additionally, keeping up OpenStack setup needs a combination of specific aptitudes. Some of these aptitudes may combine the ability to examine Python logs with respect to a key level and an understanding of network and storage as well as compute administration capabilities.

Consider combining highlights (Network, Compute, Storage or even GUI components) into the building and blueprint that cuts down the operations inconvenience. This is possible by modernizing the components setup and configurations for the part of the operations limits. Sometimes it may be helpful to use an untouchable overseeing association with dominance in administering OpenStack stable Setups of Components.

2.1.2   Failover

Despite how healthy the configuration and platform is, at some point or another administration will miss the mark. Anticipating HA can have enormous cost implications; thus the adaptability of the general production system and the individual segments will be coordinated by the necessities of the SLA to work closely all the time. Downtime masterminding consolidates making methodology and outlines that sponsorship planned (support) and impromptu (System or platform Issues) downtime.

An instance of an operational belief is the recovery of a fizzled instance. This may mean requiring the remaking of events from a review or respawning an instance on another available compute instance resource. This could have results on the general application engineering. An all-around helpful cloud platform might not need to have the ability to migrate instances beginning with one instance then onto the following available instances. If the desire is that the application will be planned to persevere through disappointment, additional examinations should be made around supporting instance movements from one to another within zero or less downtime. In this circumstance, extra supporting administrations, including shared capacity associated with compute instances, should be set.

2.1.3   Monitoring

Like other cloud platform arrangements for the setup and configurations, OpenStack requires some perfect well-being checker segments or tools to ensure any disappointments or failures are caught and mapped reasonably. Consider using any present metering and monitoring system to check whether it will have the ability to effectively check all OpenStack platforms and native components out of the box.

While there are various details and activities that should be watched, specific estimations are in a general sense vital to get consolidated images or disk utilization, or reaction time to the compute interfaces or storage or network bandwidth usage, etc.

2.1.4   Capacity Arrangement (Storage Design)

Limiting evaluation for future advancement is a fundamentally key and habitually overlooked thought. Limited impediments in an all-around valuable cloud environment consolidates compute and capacity limits of OpenStack platform. There is a relationship between the measure of the compute environment and the supporting OpenStack framework controller center points required to bolster it. As the range of the supporting image environment grows, the network action and messages will expand, which will add extra load to the controller or framework organizing centers. While no unflinching standard exists, convincing observations of the platform will help with limited measure on when to scale the back-end platform as a part of the scaling of the compute resources or storage capacities to supply required space.

Adding extra compute power to an OpenStack cloud platform is a scaling out procedure as dependable setup compute instances normally join to an OpenStack cloud platform. Know about any additional work that is relied upon to put the instances into the best and nearest accessibility zones from where compute can be associated easily. Make a point to use undefined or for all intents and purposes more CPUs while adding additional compute instances to the platform, or else live movement of the data, or migration, of the segments will break in between. Scaling out compute instances will directly impact networking components and other datacenter resources so it will be vital to incorporate resources to the farthest point or network switches/routers or other networking segments to be established in a proper way.

Another decision involves checking the ordinary workloads and development of the amount of instances that can continue running inside the compute environment by changing the overcommit extent. While only legitimate in a couple of circumstances, it's a basic thing to remember that changing the CPU overcommit extent can have a hindering effect and cause a potential augmentation in an uproarious neighbor. The extra threat of extending the overcommit extent is more instances that will miss the mark when a compute instance proclaims disappointment and your whole arrangement for the extra compute resources can create the huge capacity waste, which can incur huge costs to your organization as in capacity borrowed from the native hardware or virtualized environment platform.

Compute instance parts can in a like manner be redesigned to speak up to expansions prerequisites of the underneath resources or we can determine the native capacity of the existing setup after; this is known as vertical scaling. Redesigning CPUs with more cores, or extending the general VM memory, can incorporate extra required limits depending upon whether the running applications are more CPU raised or memory concentrated or storage intended.

Deficient plates in the farthest point could in like manner adversely influence general execution including CPU and Memory usage. Dependent upon the platform back-end configuration of the OpenStack Block Storage layer, there may be limits on adding capacity racks to corporate business-level storage structures or presenting additional block storage. It may be essential to upgrade particularly associated capacity presented in compute or add capacity to the basic storage to give additional transient storage to specific instances.

2.1.5 Architecture Considerations

Hardware Equipment choice includes three key territories:

- Compute power
- Network capacity
- Storage class

For each of these districts, the determination of equipment for an all-around helpful OpenStack cloud must reflect the way that the cloud has no pre-portrayed usage model. This infers there will be wide applications running on this cloud platform and will have fluctuating resource use necessities. A couple of utilizations will be RAM-raised, a couple of uses will be CPU-genuine, while others will be capacity concentrated. Thus, picking equipment items for an extensively helpful OpenStack cloud must give adjusted access to each and every particular resource.

Certain equipment assets structure variables may fit the bill for use in an extensively valuable OpenStack cloud platform as a consequence of the necessity for a proportional or verging on level with equality of advantages. Server parts for an all-around valuable OpenStack design layout must be proportional or measure up to conform to the compute farthest point (RAM and CPU), Network limit (number and speed of associations), and capacity limit (gigabytes or terabytes or petabytes) and moreover Incorporate IOPS.

OpenStack Server supplies are evaluated around four conflicting estimations:

2.1.5.1   Server density

A measure of what number of servers can fit into a given measure of physical space, for example, a rack unit [U].

2.1.5.2   Asset capacity

The quantity of CPU cores, the amount of RAM, or the amount of capacity as in storage with a given server will convey.

2.1.5.3   Expandability

The quantity of extra assets that can be added to a server before it has achieved its cutoff or saturation limit.

2.1.5.4   Cost

The relative given price of the hardware weighted against the level of layout effort expected to make the structure compatible.

Growing server density suggests surrendering resource limits or expandability, regardless; extending resource limits and expandability manufactures cost and decays server density. In a like manner, choosing the best server equipment item for an extensively valuable OpenStack building suggests perceiving how the choice of structure part will influence whatever is left for the setup.

- Blade servers usually support dual multi-core CPUs, which is the configuration all-around thought to be the "sweet spot" for a general reason cloud platform setup. Blades offer exceptional density. For example, both HP Blade System and Dell PowerEdge M1000e support up to 16 servers in only 10 Rack Units. In any case, the blade servers themselves now and again have confined capacity and network administration limits. Moreover, the expandability of various blade servers can be compelled.

- 1U rack-mounted servers include only a lone rack unit. Their focal points incorporate high density, support for dual socket multi-core CPUs, and backing for sensible RAM slots. This structure variable offers confined capacity limit, compelled network restraints, and limited expandability.

- 2U rack-mounted servers offer the augmented storage and network administration restrictions that 1U servers tend to require, yet with a relating reduction in server density (an expansive segment of the density offered by 1U rack-mounted servers).

- Greater rack-mounted servers, for instance, 4U servers, will tend to offer essentially more unmistakable CPU limit, oftentimes supporting four or even eight CPU sockets. These servers routinely have substantially more vital expandability so they will give the best other option to upgradability. That is to say, the servers will have a much lower server density and a great deal of more conspicuous hardware costs.

Given the wide decision of equipment parts and general customer necessities, the best shape part for the server equipment hardware supporting an all-around helpful OpenStack cloud platform is driven by outside third-party business and cost variables. No single reference designing will apply to all executions; the decision must stream out of the customer essentials, particular examinations and operational considerations. Here are some of the key elements that affect the decision of server equipment hardware:

2.1.5.4.1   Node Density

Measuring is a basic thought for an all-around valuable OpenStack cloud. The normal or expected number of events that each hypervisor can host is a commonplace metric used as a piece of assessing the setup. The picked server hardware needs to bolster the typical or expected event density.

2.1.5.4.2   Host Density

Physical server ranches have limited physical space, power, and cooling. The amount of hosts (or hypervisors) that can be fitted into a given metric (rack, rack unit, or floor tile) is another basic methodology for evaluating. Floor weight is a routinely dismissed thought. The server ranch floor must have the ability to support the weight of the proposed number of hosts inside a rack or set of racks. These elements should be associated with a component of the host density tally and server gear equipment decisions.

2.1.5.4.3   Power Density

Server farms have a predefined measure of force encouraged to a given rack or set of racks. More traditional server farms may have a power density as force as low as 20 AMPs for every rack, while later server farms can be architected to support power densities as high as 120 AMP for each rack. The chose server hardware product must consider power density.

2.1.5.4.4   Network Density

The picked server hardware must have the correct number of network affiliations and likewise the right kind of network affiliations, remembering the true objective is to bolster the proposed outline. Remember that, in any event, there are no less than two grouped system affiliations coming into each rack. For designs requiring fundamentally more abundance, it might be essential to assert that the network affiliations are from different telecom suppliers. Various server farms have that availability.

    The decision of certain structure components or outlines will impact the determination of server gear. Case in point: if the setup outline requires a scale-out capacity designing (for instance, using Ceph, Gluster, or a similar business course of action), then the server hardware decision should be carefully considered to organize the essentials set by the business game plan. Ensure that the picked server hardware is intended to bolster enough storage point of confinement (or limit expandability) to facilitate the necessities of a picked scale-out capacity plan. Case in point: if a concentrated storage game plan is required, for instance, a united storage exhibit from a capacity supplier that has InfiniBand or FDDI affiliations, the server gear should have network connector connectors acquainted with the capacity bunch vendor's particulars.

    Correspondingly, the network building will influence the server equipment item determination in a different way. Case in point: guarantee that the server is composed with enough additional framework ports and augmentation cards to support most of the networks required. There is variability in network extension cards, so it is crucial to think about potential impacts or limitations issues with various parts in the configuration. This is especially substantial if the configuration uses InfiniBand or another less used network administration tradition convention.

2.1.6   Choosing Storage Equipment

Like the case with capacity building, selecting a network plan as often as possible makes sense of which system hardware will be used. The Networking programs being utilized are directed by the picked sorting out gear. Some arrangement impacts are plainly obvious; for example, selecting organizing gear that solitary sponsorships Gigabit Ethernet (GbE) will really influence an extensive variety of districts of the general diagram. So likewise, picking 10 Gigabit Ethernet (10 GbE) affects distinctive locales of the general setup outline.

For example, selecting Cisco Networking hardware proposes that the designing will use Cisco Networking programming like IOS or NX-OS. Then again, selecting Arista Networking gear suggests the network contraptions will use the Arista Networking programming called Extensible Operating Software (EOS). Besides these, there are more unpretentious layout influences that ought to be considered. The decision of certain Networking hardware (and consequently the system programming) could impact the organization instruments that can be used. There are unique cases to this; the climb of "open" network programming that support an extent of systems administration hardware suggests that there are events where the relationship between network administration gear and network administration programs are not as immovably portrayed. An instance of this sort of writing computer programs is Cumulus Linux, which is fit for running on different switch dealers' equipment courses of action.

A bit of the key thoughts that should be fused into the decision of network administration gear include:

2.1.6.1   Port Count

The configuration will require networking equipment that has the essential port count.

2.1.6.2   Port Density

The network setup will be impacted by the physical space that is required to give the vital port number. A switch that can supply 48 10 GbE ports in 1U has a much higher port density than a switch that gives 24 10 GbE ports in 2U. A higher port density is very favored, as it leaves more rack space for compute or capacity sections that may be required by the design. This can similarly lead to stress over imperfect regions and power density that should be considered. Higher density switches are costlier and should be considered, as it is fundamental not to overdesign the network if it is not required.

2.1.6.3   Port Speed

The networking equipment must be backing up the proposed network speed, for instance: 1 GbE, 10 GbE, or 40 GbE (or even 100 GbE).

2.1.6.4   Redundancy

The level of network excess hardware required is influenced by the customer requirements for high accessibility and cost thoughts. Excess networks can be refined by including redundant power supplies or switches. If this is an essential, the gear ought to bolster the platform plan. Customer essentials will make sense of whether an absolute excess framework base is required.

2.1.6.5   Power Necessities

Guarantee that the genuine server-farm core supplies the indispensable power for the picked system gear. This is not a case for top-of-rack (ToR) switches, yet it may be a case for spine switches in a leaf and spine fabric, or end of row (EoR) switches.

There is no one best practice plan for the network gear supporting a generally helpful OpenStack cloud platform that will apply to all setups. A segment of the key parts that will influence decisions of network administration hardware include:

2.1.6.6 Network Connectivity

All instances inside an OpenStack cloud platform need some kind of framework association. From time to time, they must oblige access to more than one framework segment. The outline must join a satisfactory framework and transmission capacity to ensure that all exchanges inside the cloud platform, both north-south and east-west action have adequate resources available.

2.1.6.7 Versatility

The picked network framework layout should fuse a physical and clever framework arrangement that can be easily created/altered. A network framework should offer the sorts of interfaces and speeds that are required by the gear instances to communicate with other components.

2.1.6.8 Accessibility

To ensure that approval to platform instances inside the cloud is not meddled with, it is recommended that the network framework plan recognizes any single reasons for disillusionment and give some level of excess or adjustment to interior disappointment. With respect to the network framework establishment itself, this frequently includes usage of network traditions, for instance, LACP, VR-RP or others to achieve an uncommonly open network framework association. In a like manner, it is imperative to consider the networks administration repercussions on programming interface availability. In order to make certainty that the APIs, and perhaps distinctive administrations in the cloud are exceptionally open and accessible, it is suggested to blueprint load adjusting courses of action inside the network design to oblige for these necessities.

2.1.7 Choice of Applications

Programming choices for a universally useful OpenStack engineering plan needs to incorporate these three zones:

- Working framework (OS) and hypervisor

- OpenStack parts

- Supplemental application

The decision of working structures including OS and hypervisor enormously influences the worldwide cloud platform plot. Picking a particular working system and hypervisor can moreover direct impact server hardware choice. It is suggested to guarantee the capacity equipment decision and topology bolster the picked working system and hypervisor mix. Finally, ensure that the systems administration hardware determination and topology will work with the picked working structure and hypervisor mix. Case in point: if the outline arrangement uses Link Aggregation Control Protocol (LACP), the OS and hypervisor both have to support it.

A couple of ranges that could be influenced by the decision of OS and hypervisor include:

2.1.7.1 Pricing

Selecting a monetarily maintained hypervisor, for instance, Microsoft Hyper-V, will realize another cost show instead of group reinforced open source hypervisors including KVM, Kinstance, or Xen. When choosing open source OS courses of action, picking Ubuntu over Red Hat (or a different way) cost as a result of support contracts. Of course, business or application necessities may deal with a specific or monetarily upheld hypervisor.

2.1.7.2   Support

Dependent upon the picked hypervisor, the staff should have the best possible way to get ready and figure out how to bolster the picked OS and hypervisor blend. In case they don't, have another option ready, but this could have a cost impact on the layout.

2.1.7.3   Administration tools and techniques

The association administration devices used for Ubuntu and Kinstance contrast from the organization gadgets for VMware vSphere. Yet both OS and hypervisor mixes are upheld by OpenStack; there will be particularly diverse impacts on whatever is left of the layout as a delayed consequence of the determination of one blend versus the other.

2.1.7.4   Scale and Execution

Ensure that picked OS and hypervisor blends meet the appropriate scale and execution necessities. The picked outline should meet the concentrated on-event host extents with the picked OS-hypervisor mixes.

2.1.7.5   Security

Ensure that the design can suit the steady incidental foundation of utilization security patches while keeping up the required workloads. The repeat of security patches for the proposed OS-hypervisor mix will influence execution, and the patch foundation strategy could impact support windows.

2.1.7.6   Upheld highlights

Make sense of which components of OpenStack are required. This will frequently help make the decision of the OS-hypervisor mix. Certain components are only available with specific OSs or hypervisors.

2.1.7.7   Interoperability

Thought should be given to the ability of the picked OS-hypervisor mix to interoperate or exist together with various OS-hypervisors and what other programming game plans in the general diagram (it truly needs). Operational examination of virtual products for one OS-hypervisor blend may change from the instruments used for another OS-hypervisor mix and, as need be, the outline design ought to address if the two courses of action of devices require them to interoperate.

2.1.8   OpenStack parts

The determination of which OpenStack parts are fused altogether influences the general outline arrangement. While there are certain fragments that will reliably be accessible (Compute and Image Service, for example), there are distinctive administrations that may not be required. For example, a particular configuration outline won't require Orchestration. Disposing of Orchestration would not essentially influence the general arrangement of a cloud platform; in any case, if the building uses a trade for OpenStack Object storage for its storage part, it could possibly influence whatever is left of the configuration layout.

The shirking of certain OpenStack portions may keep or force the convenience of various parts. If the designing joins coordination yet restricts Telemetry, then the setup won't have the ability to endeavor Orchestrations' autoscaling value (which relies on upon information from Telemetry). It is basic procedure to ask about the fragment interdependencies in conjunction with the particular necessities before picking what sections should be fused and what portions can be dropped from the last stable design outline.

2.1.9   Supplemental parts

While OpenStack is a really complete amassing of programming assignments for building a phase for cloud services, there are additional bits of programming that should be considered in any given OpenStack outline to build robust cloud platforms.

2.1.9.1   Networking aspects

OpenStack Networking has a wide accumulation of Network association for instances. There are different extra network services application programming bunches that may be valuable to deal with the OpenStack segments themselves.

For a thoroughly profitable OpenStack cloud platform, the OpenStack foundation segments should be altogether accessible. In the event that the configuration bars hardware LB, arranging applications packs like HAProxy should be merged.

2.1.9.2   Monitoring segments

The picked supplemental application strategy effects on the general OpenStack cloud game plan. This controlled programming for giving clustering, logging, monitoring and alarming.

Considered bunching applications, for example, Corosync or Pacemaker, is stay away from mined in a general sense by the openness necessities. Along these lines, the effect of including (or excepting) these thing clusters is principally picked by the accessibility of the cloud foundation and the multifaceted method for supporting the game plan after it is set up. The OpenStack High Availability Guide gives subtler segments on the foundation and plan of Corosync and Pacemaker, and these gatherings should be combined into the blueprint outline.

Necessities for logging, monitoring, and cautioning are controlled by operational contemplations. Each of these subclasses solidifies distinctive different decision makers. For example, in the logging sub-gathering one should consider Logstash, Splunk, instanceware Log Insight, or some other log cementing application. Logs should be secured in a joined locale to make it less perplexing to perform examination against the data. Log data examination engines can, in a like way, give robotization and issue forewarning by giving a method to both alarms and endeavor to remediate a section of the regularly known issues.

On the off chance that any of these item bundles are required, then the system must record for the extra favorable position use (CPU, RAM, storage, and structure data transmission for a log gathering course of action, for event). Some other potential design course of action impacts include the following:

- OS-hypervisor combination: Guarantee that the chosen logging, screening, or alarming apparatuses support the proposed OS-hypervisor combination.

- Network system hardware: The system equipment choice should be supported by the logging, screening, and alarming applications.

2.1.9.3   Database components

A bigger part of the OpenStack pieces oblige access to back-end database administrations to store state and data for the segments of OpenStack and users. Assurance of a sensible back-end database that will fulfill the openness and acclimation to nonfundamental dissatisfaction necessities of the OpenStack administrations is required. OpenStack administrations bolsters interfacing with any database that is kept up by the local SQLAlchemy Python drivers, regardless; the broadest database administrations make utilization of MySQL or combinations of it. It is supported that the database that gives back-end administrations inside an overall accommodating cloud be made uncommonly open while utilizing an accessible improvement that can finish that objective. A section of the more vital application programming courses of action utilized join Galera, MariaDB, and MySQL with Master replication.

2.1.9.4   Tending to execution touchy workloads

However, one of the key depicting portions for a broadly important OpenStack cloud platform is that execution is not a picking variable; there may at present some execution unstable workloads went on the inside and out supportive OpenStack cloud platform.

2.1.9.5   Compute centric workloads

In an OpenStack cloud platform that is compute centered, there are some structure decisions that can oblige workloads. Compute centered workloads are by and large that would put a higher burden on CPU and memory assets with lower need given as far as possible and system execution, other than what is required to strengthen the proposed compute workloads.

2.1.9.6   Network centric workloads

In a network system centered OpenStack cloud platform, some design setup decisions can enhance the execution of workloads. System centered workloads persuading requesting on System transmission capacity speed and maintained administrations that require particular thoughts and plan.

2.1.9.7   Storage capacity centric workloads

Capacity limit centered OpenStack cloud platforms should be proposed to oblige workloads that have persuading solicitations on either object or block storage administrations that require specific thoughts and sorting out.

2.1.10   Real-time example

An online portal affiliation needs to run web applications containing Glassfish, HAProxy, and Percona XtraDB Group in a private cloud platform. With a specific goal to meet arrangement essentials, the cloud base will keep running in its own particular data focus. The portal will have clear weight essentials yet require a portion of scaling to change in accordance with consistent increments. The present setup is not sufficiently adaptable to adjust the objective of running an open source programming interface driven environment. A present domain incorporates the running with:

- Somewhere around 240 and 280 node setup of HAProxy and Glassfish, each with 4 vCPU and 8 GB of RAM.

- A three-node Percona XtraDB Cluster, each with 8 vCPUs and 16 GB RAM.

The application runs part-based LBs and different web applications serving the regions. The affiliation composes their surroundings utilizing a blend of bash scripts and Ansible. The goals make a lot of log information reliable that should be chronicled. The arrangement would comprise the accompanying OpenStack parts:

- A firewall, switches, and load balancers on general confronting network associations.

- OpenStack Controller administrations running image, identity, networking, and supporting administrations: for example, MySQL and ActiveMQ. The controllers will keep running in an exceptionally accessible arrangement on no less than three controller hosts.

- OpenStack Compute hosts running the KVM hypervisors.

- OpenStack Block Storage for use by compute nodes that require diligent storage, for example, databases for dynamic web applications.

- OpenStack Object Storage for serving static contents, for example, pictures and static web portal content.

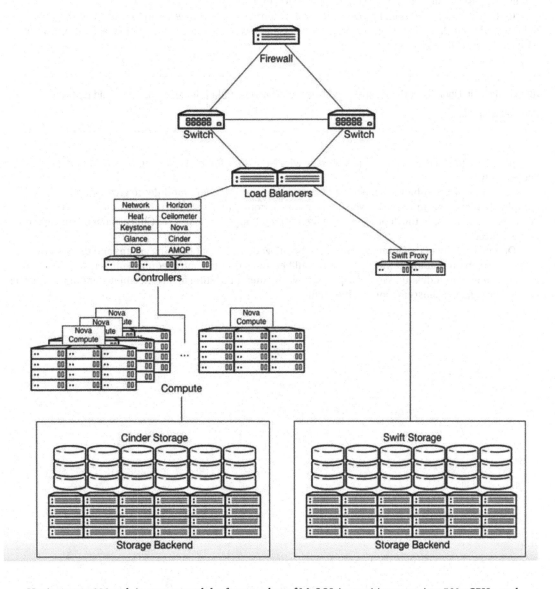

Having up to 280 web instances and the few number of MySQL in-positions requires 560 vCPUs, and 1120 GB RAM. On an average 1U server with dual core hex-center Intel CPUs with Hyper threading, and enduring 2:1 CPU overcommit ratio enabled, this would require 16 OpenStack Compute instances for a given situation.

The web application instances will keep running from adjacent available storage on each of the OpenStack Compute instances. The web application instances can be stateless, meaning that any of the cases can come up short and still the application will keep working.

MySQL server instances store their information on shared undertaking storage, for example, NetApp or Solidfire gadgets. In the event that a MySQL instance comes up short, Storage would be relied on to be rejoined to another instance and rejoined to the Percona XtraDB Group. Logs from the web application servers are passed onto OpenStack Object Storage for analysis.

In this condition, additional capacity of confinement can be perceived by moving static web substance to be served from OpenStack Object storage holders, and fortification the OpenStack Image Administration with OpenStack Object storage.

An expansion in OpenStack Object storage implies that Network data transfer capacity should be taken into consideration.

It is better to run OpenStack Object Storage with Network affiliations offering 10 GbE or better accessibility.

There is also a credibility to affect the Orchestration and Telemetry modules to give an autoscaling, completely developed and oversee web application environment. Depicting the web applications in Heat Formats would discredit the dependence on the scripted Puppet or Ansible or Chef arrangements right now being utilized.

OpenStack Networking administration can be utilized to control LBs using groups and the Systems Administration programming interface. This would permit a user to control equipment load leveling pools and occurrences as individuals in these pools; however their utilization in advancement conditions must be precisely weighed against current reliable quality.

CHAPTER 3

■ ■ ■

OpenStack Deployment

Setting up and configuring an OpenStack platform in light of the profiled outline, as in the past chapter, is not straightforward. Despite the fact that we made our configuration by dealing with a few viewpoints identified with adaptability and execution, we still need to make it genuine.

Besides, in the initial segment of this book, we secured the place of OpenStack in the up-and-coming era of datacenters. The base has now ended up programmable through APIs. In any case, an expansive scale base utilized by cloud suppliers needs an altogether different methodology so as to set it up with a couple of thousand servers.

For our situation, conveying and working with the OpenStack Cloud platform is not as basic as you may think. However, you should enjoy some good times by just having fun and playing around with it. You have to make any operational undertaking less demanding or, at the end of the day, mechanized. Surprisingly, OpenStack is not a complete cloud working framework. Keep in mind that it may get to be one after some time, but it's presumably best to consider at OpenStack as a kernel, not an OS.

With a specific end goal – to end up broadly received by the venture, OpenStack should at last be conveyed by means of vigorous, endeavor-level items that narrow the gap of the key territories where OpenStack has challenges. These items are conveyed today by organizations that bolster, simplify, and establish instruments for everyday administration, and the greater part of alternate pieces essential for accomplishing acknowledgment. Without these merchants who have a stake in big business selection, OpenStack can never be generally deployed as a cloud platform. OpenStack isn't a relational or nonrelational database system. It's the complete Linux including kernel and hardware and applications; and like the Linux piece, you require a complete working framework like OS to make it work.

There are some key characteristics that are highly related with OpenStack post-deployment and pre-deployments.

- Uptime of APIs and Versatile Controlling parts

- Powerful Administration and Security Models

- Open Engineering of platform design

- Cloud Interoperability

- Versatile and Flexible Engineering design

- Worldwide Backing and Administration services

- Mechanization/Automation

I will characterize the above-mentioned items one by one. As a key step in beginning, let's take a look at OpenStack's place in the venture.

3.1   OpenStack in the Venture Server-Farm

Speed is the new watchword for cloud, and DevOps is seen as the way to acknowledge speed. OpenStack gives the perfect stage to convey another programming experience inside the undertaking organization, pretty much as Linux gave another experience to web applications and Web appropriation. On the off chance that OpenStack was only a "less expensive enterprise cloud platform vendor," then it would have aligned to zero worth to the organization. Rather, OpenStack gives a sparkling case of how to set up a private versatile cloud like real open clouds, for example, AWS and VMWare. Generally, as Hadoop brought Google's MapReduce (in addition to its reference design engineering) to the masses, OpenStack brings the AWS/GCP-style IaaS offering to everybody. This is the thing that makes DevOps inside the undertaking organization at last sparkle.

The keyword DevOps is a conjunction of advancement (program designers) and operations (oversee and place programming into live systems). Numerous IT associations have begun to receive such an idea, yet the question is how and what? Does it work? Is it a procedure or a piece of ITIL implementation practices?

DevOps is a development and operations compound, which essentially characterizes an SDLC improvement. It portrays implementations that streamline the product conveyance process. And this is not all. Indeed, it is more about raising correspondence and combination between developers, administrators (counting heads), and quality affirmation. The quintessence of the DevOps development is in the advantages of coordinated effort. Distinctive controls can identify with DevOps and bring their encounters and aptitudes together under the DevOps mark to assemble a front of shared qualities. Any discourse about DevOps, similar a hefty portion of the late trendy expressions, can rapidly get to be buried in semantic contentions. Notwithstanding, the one axiom we would all be able to concur on is that the conventional obstructions between application engineers and IT framework administrators should be broken.

Over and over, I hear comparative stories from our clients that go this way: "We went to the platform provider groups with our considerable rundown of prerequisites for our new application venture. They replied it would take around 22 months or so and $15M before it would be prepared. So we went to publicly available largest platform provider, so-called AWS. We didn't get our desired framework necessities and we needed to change our application model as per the platform, yet we got the opportunity to advertise promptly." That is on the grounds that the inborn estimation of AWS has less to do with expense and more to do with the on-interest, versatile and engineer-driven conveyance model."

OpenStack makes everything fair inside the endeavor. Private cloud platform can be based on a general cloud model, empowering engineers while giving unified IT control and administration. Fundamentally, it's the best of both universes, which is the genuine estimation of OpenStack-controlled private cloud platform.

3.2   Why Does Speed Make a Difference?

By far, most of the new applications are centered around making businesses held in esteem, commonly around IoT, mobile, social, web applications, and analytics. Indeed, this class of utilization is developing so quickly that examiners, for example, IDC and Gartner, have begun following it.

Table 3-1. *Application Growth Table*

Applications		Traditional	Modern
Name		SAP, App Dynamics, Java	Cassandra, Hadoop, NodeJS
Year	2012	89M	5M
	2015	139M	32M
Growth		56%	540%

Cutting-edge applications are the hotspot for future aggressiveness for most undertakings, which has driven them to quicken their cloud selection process and reevaluate their cloud system as mentioned in Application growth table. We have now entered an "adjust or kick the minute" for undertakings, and OpenStack will be vital to speed adjustment and the fruitful backing of DevOps. Let's dive deeply to the core characteristics that I mentioned earlier for deployment requirements step by step.

3.3 Uptime of APIs and Versatile Controlling Part

We have now entered an "adjust or kick the time" for organizations phase, and here OpenStack will be vital to speed the adoption and the fruitful backing of DevOps.

3.3.1 OpenStack API Uptime and Accessibility

A basic ability for moving to another cloud platform and DevOps model is the capacity of cloud-local applications to a course of failures in a flexible cloud platform. These applications realize that any given server, drive, or network gadget could stop working at any point in time. They search for these disappointments and handle them progressively in real time. That is the way AWS and Google Cloud run and why they can run these administrations/managing in an effortlessly structured manner and with more noteworthy adaptability. For an application to adjust progressively to the typical disappointments of individual segments, the cloud APIs must have higher-than-ordinary accessibility.

3.3.2 Platform Controller Throughput

Programming interface uptime isn't the main estimation of progress. Your platform control plane throughput is likewise basic. Think about the control plane as the war room of your cloud platform as it depends on your networking and routing mechanisms. It is the vast majority of the centralized knowledge and orchestration layer. Your APIs are a subset of the control plane, which for OpenStack likewise incorporates all of center OpenStack ventures, your everyday cloud administration programming or application development (as a thumb-rule part of a seller's Endeavor grade OpenStack dissemination), and the greater part of the subordinate administrations/management required – for example, databases, OpenStack merchant modules, and so forth. Your cloud control plane requires scaling as your cloud becomes larger and larger. This implies that in total, you have more aggregate throughput for Programming interface operations (object push/pull, image transfer/downloads, and so on.).

3.3.3 API Uptime and Scaling Controller Plane

As the vast majority of you know, conveying 99.999% of accessibility is a non-inconsequential errand, as this is just 5.24 minutes of impromptu downtime permitted every year. Average high accessibility methodologies, for example, active/passive or expert election frameworks, can take a few minutes to failover, leaving your cloud Programming interface endpoints distracted.

A venture-grade cloud working framework can give sureties of sub-moment or even sub-second failover and convey 99.999% or potentially even 99.9999% uptime. This sort of configuration is achievable at a moderately low value point utilizing exemplary load adjusting style strategies.

You are required to control the plane to develop as your cloud platform develops. You would prefer not to re-draft your framework as it develops, and you would prefer not to turn to old-fashioned scaling procedures for your Programming interface endpoints. When you run active/passive or with a master election framework for HA, a stand-out Programming interface endpoint is accessible at once. That implies that you are essentially bottlenecked by the aggregate throughput of a solitary server, which is inadmissible in today's scaling cloud platform provider world.

3.4   Powerful Administration and Security Models

You presumably know this as of now, yet assembling a vigorous, sensible, and secure framework for infrastructure in the undertaking organization isn't simple. The thought that private cloud platform can be conveyed in an evening and underway that night doesn't wash with the substances of the datacenter. Still, time is of the utmost and in the event that you need a cloud platform that doesn't need to be updated and you need it (moderately) quick, then it will be an easy case if the flavor of OpenStack that you pick has been already outlined in terms of arrangement, day-by-day administration, and security. How about we investigate what that involves? Let's start with the block of management.

3.4.1   Powerful Administration

Setup is just the starting with regard to overseeing management of OpenStack Cloud platform. A genuine cloud platform OS gives a suite of administrator-driven cloud administration applications intended to permit the core datacenter or infrastructure admin group or platform admins to be fruitful at administration conveyance and delivery of platform. These administration applications serve:

- Repeatable compositional design model, ideally utilizing chunks wired together with a reference topology design

- Introductory cloud platform setup and configuration

- As a routine, cloud administrator apparatuses for logging, framework measurements, and connection

- Platform administrator CLI and Programming interface for joining and mechanization

- Platform administrator GUI for perception and investigation

Numerous endeavors to comprehend the private cloud administration challenges stop at setting up. Setting up the platform can be the only starting point of your trip, and how simple it is doesn't make a difference if your cloud is then difficult to maintain on an hourly or daily basis. As all know, running a live operational framework is difficult. If the truth be told, private cloud platforms are altogether more mind boggling than customary infrastructure foundation approaches in numerous ways. To resolve the failures, at scale, the cloud pioneers, for example, Google, Amazon, and Facebook have all managed a clusters, pods, or blocks-based way to deal with planning, setup, and dealing with their cloud platform. Google adopted clusters; Facebook works with triplets; however, it's all at last the same: A Lego block-like repeatable way to deal with setting up your cloud platform and datacenter. World-class OpenStack-controlled cloud OS frameworks should give a comparative way to deal with cloud association.

Once the private cloud platform has been up and working fine, administrators of cloud require some of applications or software to keep up the cloud platform all the time, including processing of system metrics logs and OS measurements. Certainly, in a flexible cloud processing that used to be basic (e.g., server or switch disappointment) are needed no more. In any case, your cloud platform can't be a black box. You require data on how it's working every day so you can investigate particular issues as required and, above all, watch out for repeating issues utilizing relationship applications. An individual server disappointment will always be an issue. However, for any sort of regular issue that is viable, a lot of assets should be searched out and immediately tended to.

What's happening with your cloud platform? Don't you have to know, as well as your different applications and platform groups may need to know too? Joining to existing frameworks is basic to wide selection. Any complete arrangement will have a Programming interface and command-line interface to permit you to coordinate and computerize. A CLI and Programming interface for just OpenStack regulatory necessities is insufficient. Shouldn't something be said about your physical server plant or administration of your pieces or cases? What about having the capacity to recover framework measurements and logging information on interest from OpenStack, as well as Linux and other non-OpenStack applications? You require a solitary, bound-together interface for cloud operations and administration. Clearly, in the event that you have this Programming interface, a GUI ought to likewise be accommodated for those extraordinary cloud administrator undertakings that require perceptions, for example, searching for examples in framework and system measurements.

3.4.2   Security

Cloud platform turns the security model on its head. A complete examination of this subject is a long way past this chapter, yet endeavors need a private cloud with a reasonable security model, especially for the control plane. As we secured in the past portion of this arrangement, your cloud control plane's Programming interface uptime and throughput is basic to permitting cutting-edge applications to course around inconveniently. Thus, the security of your cloud's control plane ought not to be underestimated.

It can be anything but difficult to become involved with the move toward a decentralized model; however decentralized and scaling out are not the same thing. You can really blend centralization and scaling methods and this is the genuine approach that cloud pioneer Google employs. Keeping your cloud control plane in one spot permits you to do the following:

- Have a solitary go-to area for debugging and resolution

- Continuously know where your control plane is found instead of guessing

- Apply security approaches to your control plane

- Keep your control plane information totally isolated from plane information

You don't need your OpenStack database to dwell on the same storage framework as your VMs. Consider the possibility that somebody breaks into a VM through the hypervisor. On the other hand, alternately, what happens on the off chance that somebody breaks into the control plane through a Programming interface?

Best practices in the undertaking have, since a long time ago, contained a methodology of zoning of various parts into various security regions with varying arrangements connected. Zoning backs an aggressor off, gives you an opportunity to recognize them, and to react. Having the capacity to take a comparative approach to deal with your private cloud security model is indispensable to making certain your cloud is secure.

3.4.3   Cloud Administration and Security

Your excursion starts with the establishment of the cloud platform. After that, you require an arrangement of applications/software and a security model that permits you to certainly deal with your cloud platform step by step. An Undertaking grade, OpenStack-fueled cloud working framework should convey however much of these abilities as could be expected.

OpenStack is a solid establishment for building a cutting-edge private cloud intended for cutting-edge cloud applications. Happily, it is almost finished cloud working framework and but you may require an accomplice to give you that arrangement.

3.5 Open Engineering of Platform Design

We officially secured fabricating a powerful control plane and cloud administration framework. One of the attractions of OpenStack is expelling seller lock-in by moving to an open source stage. This is a key quality suggestion and merits a complete exchange about what is sensible and what is not in a venture of OpenStack.

Are you being guaranteed that OpenStack gives "no lock-in?" No merchant lock-in is a dispassionate perfect - something that can be envisioned as an impeccable structure, however never accomplished. Any framework dependably has some type of lock-in. For instance, a large number of you most likely utilize RHEL, a totally 100% open source Linux OS framework, as your default Linux inside your business. However, RHEL is a type of lock-in. RHEL is a particular form of Linux intended for a particular objective. You are bolted into their specific reference engineering, bundling frameworks, installers/bootloaders, and so on, despite the fact that it is open source.

Actually, with numerous clients I have seen to a lesser degree an apprehension about lock-in and to a greater extent a worry about being "more secure." For instance, one client, who will stay anonymous, was worried about embracing our block storage segment, despite the fact that it was 100% open source because of lock-in concerns. Whenever examined, it turned out to be clear that what the client needed was to utilize their current storage sellers (NetApp and Hitachi Data Frameworks) and did not have any desire to need to prepare their IT groups on a totally new capacity capability. Here the lock-in concerns were overwhelmingly about engrossing more security as opposed to expelling it.

What is most vital is evaluating the dangers your business can take. Moving to OpenStack, as with Linux before it, implies that you are relieving sure dangers regarding preparing your IT groups on the new platform framework and supporting your wagers by having the capacity to get various sellers in-house to bolster your open source programming.

At the end of the day, OpenStack can unquestionably diminish lock-in, however it won't expel it. Along these lines, request an open design, yet expect an undertaking platform product.

3.5.1 Lock-in Happens, Especially with Big Business Items

I wish it didn't, yet lock-in happens, as should be obvious from above. That implies that as opposed to making arrangements for no lock-in, begin getting ready for what lock-in you are OK with. An undertaking of OpenStack will give an assortment of alternatives through an open design so you can fence your wagers. Be that as it may, a genuine cloud working framework and endeavor item can't ever give a vast assortment of choices. Why not? Since then the bolster model is not practical and that seller leaves business. Not even the biggest sellers can give all choices to all individuals.

In the event that you need to construct your own altered cloud working system worked around OpenStack, proceed; yet that isn't an item. That is an altered proficient administrations way. Like the individuals who moved their own Linux appropriations for some time, it prompts a way of disarray and kingdom fabrication that is terrible for your business. Doing it without anyone's help is likewise asset concentrated. You'll need 30-35 Python designers with a profound learning of foundation (compute, storage, and network) who can hack full time on your degraded OpenStack. A group that looks something like this:

Table 3-2. *Resources requirements*

Asset Sort	Least Responsibility
Hypervisor Vendor	3
Hypervisor Expert	3
Storage Vendor	3
Storage Expert	3
Network Vendor	3
Network Expert	3
DevOps Expert	3
Linux Kernel Developers	5
OpenStack Developers	5
QA	4
Total	**35**

In mentioned in Resource requirements table, at last, you must pick a seller to wager on the off chance that you need undertaking OpenStack-controlled cloud arrangements.

3.6   Cloud Interoperability

Hybrid is the new cloud platform. Most clients we converse with recognize the truth of expecting to furnish their engineers with the most ideally equipped device for the employment. Needs shift, prerequisites change, concerns fluctuate, consistency differs. Each endeavor is somewhat extraordinary. Some have to begin on open cloud, however then move to private cover after some time. Some have to begin on private, but they gradually embrace open. Some begin on both at the same time.

3.6.1   A Hybrid Cloud Procedure

Each endeavor needs a cross-cloud technique. Meaning, custom cloud ought to be your first and essential necessity. At that point, planning around cross with a solitary bound-together administration conveys the best of both worlds for your electorates. At long last, arrangement on a procedure where you will triage your applications/needs and figure out which cloud is a good fit for the employment.

3.6.1.1   Understanding Cloud Interoperability and Its Part in Hybrid Cloud

I have been through a significant number of interoperability endeavors, the most agonizing of which was IPSEC for VPNs. Interoperability between sellers is not free, as a rule requires a genuinely genuine exertion, and at last is justified regardless of the torment. Tragically, interoperability is profoundly misconstrued, especially as it applies to open/private/hybrid cloud.

The test in hybrid cloud is about tending to the issues of use compactness. On the off chance that you need a mix of open and private clouds (mixture) where an application can be sent on either cloud, moved between the clouds, starting with one cloud then onto the next, then application versatility is required. When you get and move an application and its cloud-local mechanization system starting with one cloud then onto the next, various key things need to continue as before:

- Execution must be at relatively equal

- Fundamental system, storage, and compute structures must be the same or comparative

- Your mechanization system must bolster Programming interface similarity with both clouds

- The TCO of setting the application must be inside 1/2-2x of each other

- There must be behavioral similarity, which means non-Programming interface "components" are coordinated

- You should bolster Programming interface similarity with the significant open clouds

Obviously, you should likewise have been mindful when outlining your application and dodged any lock-in elements of a specific cloud framework, for example, a dependence on DynamoDB on AWS, HA/DRS on VMware, iRules on F5 load balancers, and so on.

On the off chance that you don't meet these prerequisites, interoperability is unrealistic and application compactness endeavors will come up short. The application execution will be significantly distinctive and one cloud will be favored; there will be missed highlights that cause the application to not work on some cloud; and your robotization system may fall flat if behavioral similarity doesn't exist. For instance, maybe it has clocks in it that accept a VM comes up in 30 minutes, yet on one of your clouds it takes 1-2 hours.

These issues must be tended to, keeping in mind the end goal to accomplish crossover cloud interoperability.

3.6.1.2   OpenStack Needs a Reference Design

The Linux part requires a reference design. Actually, every real dissemination of Linux basically makes its own reference design and now we have particular kinds of Linux OS. For instance, there are the RedHat/Fedora/CentOS families and the Debian/Ubuntu families. These complete x86 working frameworks have completely prepared reference designs and anybody moving inside one of the gatherings will discover it moderately unimportant to move between them. Though a RedHat administrator moving to Debian may at first be lost until they come up to speed on the distinctions, OpenStack is the same.

OpenStack, and in reality the greater part of its open source brethren, has no reference engineering. OpenStack is truly the part for a cloud working framework. This is really its strong quality and its shortcoming. The same holds for Linux. You can get Cray Linux for a supercomputer and you can get Android for an inserted ARM gadget. Both are Linux, yet both have drastically distinctive structures, making application movability unimaginable. OpenStack is comparable, in that to date most OpenStack clouds are not interoperable, in light of the fact that each has its own particular reference engineering. Each cloud with its own reference design is destined to be an OpenSnowFlake.

Venture-based cloud working frameworks fueled by OpenStack must have normally held reference models. That way you can be guaranteed that each organization is interoperable with each other's arrangement. These reference structures have yet to emerge. Be that as it may, given that there is as of now solitary reference engineering in AWS and GCP, and given that these two organizations will be real powers out in the open cloud, it's difficult to perceive how OpenStack can abstain from supporting no less than one reference engineering that resembles the AWS/GCP model.

To be clear, be that as it may, there might be various winning reference structures. I see developing flavors in HPC and conceivably different verticals like oil and gas.

In the event that undertakings wish nimbleness, adaptability, and decision, it appears glaringly evident that OpenStack needs to bolster a venture reference design that is centered on building hybrid clouds with a definitive champ in broad public cloud. It's simply my feeling, yet at this moment that looks like Amazon, Google, and Microsoft.

Venture-based OpenStack implies an endeavor reference engineering that empowers hybrid cloud interoperability and application compactness.

An open engineering intended for hybrid cloud interoperability is an inescapable result now. Generally what people contend about is the means by which that will be accomplished; however for those of us who are logical thinkers, it's sure that open cloud will have a wide assortment of victors and that the main 10 open cloud is as of now ruled by non-OpenStack contenders. So arrange in a like manner.

In particular, remember to request open engineering, while expecting an undertaking item.

3.7   Versatile and Flexible Engineering Design

Undertaking companies needs to mean something. Previously, undertaking companies identified with a specific nature of a framework that made it very dependable, versatile, and performant. To an ever-increasing extent, undertaking evaluation is starting to signify "cloud-based" or "web scale." What I mean by that will be that as the move to cutting-edge applications happens and ventures embrace another IT model, we will see significant changes in the necessities for conveying an astounding framework.

The illustration I want to utilize is Hadoop. Hadoop accompanies a reference design that says this: use product servers, commodity disk drives, and NO RAID. At this point, when is the last time you saw an undertaking base arrangement without any information security at the equipment layer? Obviously, it doesn't bode well to run Hadoop on top of the line blades connected to a fiber channel SAN, despite the fact that I have seen it. Indeed, even Microsoft Exchange has started prescribing a move toward JBODs from RAID and relying upon the application programming layer to course around disappointment.

Versatility is the property of a framework to keep on working as it increments in size and workload requests. Execution is the estimation of the throughput of an individual asset of the framework as opposed to the framework itself.

From numerous points of view, OpenStack itself is an exceedingly adaptable framework. It was composed around an approximately coupled, message-passing design – something reliable for mid to substantial scale, while additionally ready to downsize to much smaller size organizations. The issue, lamentably, lies in what plan choices you made while arranging and sending OpenStack. Some of its default arrangements and a significant number of the merchant modules and arrangements have not been outlined in view of scale. When you read the past portion, you comprehended that having reference engineering is basic to conveying hybrid cloud. Verify that you pick an undertaking item with a reference design that thinks about scale and execution while utilizing all-around reviewed parts and arrangement decisions.

A complete examination of the scale and execution issues that may emerge with OpenStack is past the extent of this arrangement; notwithstanding, we should handle the main issue that a great many people keep running into: system execution and versatility.

3.7.1   OpenStack Default Networking Administration Bust

OpenStack Nova has three inherent default organizing models: flat, single_host, and multi_host. Every one of the three of these administration models is totally unsuitable for general ventures. Notwithstanding these default organizing models, you have the choice of sending OpenStack Neutron, which has an exceptionally pluggable design that backs various distinctive merchant modules both to oversee physical gadgets and to arrange virtualization frameworks (supposed SDN).

An exceptionally concise clarification of the default organizing models inadequacies is all together. The level and multi_host organizing model requires a solitary shared VLAN for all flexible IP addresses. This requires running STP over your switch fabric, a famously unsafe methodology on the off chance that you need high system uptime.

Maybe all the more essential, both flat and multi_host models oblige you to course your open IP addresses from your system edge down to the hypervisor hubs. This is truly not an adequate methodology in any current venture.

Likewise, it's likely important that on the off chance that you need multi_host mode, you should have the capacity to load code on your hypervisor. That implies in the event that you like ESX or Hyper-V you are presumably in a tough situation.

By differentiation, single_host mode experiences the particular sin of attempting to make a solitary x86 server the center Networking point through which all activity among VLANs and the Web runs. Essentially, take your superior switch fabric and toss it in the garbage on the grounds that your most extreme data transfer capacity is whatever a Linux server can push. Once more, this is not an adequate or even valid way to deal with Networking systems.

These methodologies have crucial versatility and execution issues – which conveys us to OpenStack Neutron.

3.7.2 Contingent upon OpenStack Neutron NOT for the Weak of Heart

Without a reference network system engineering, your capacity to scale past a solitary rack is simply taking into account hand-waving and confirmations from your seller that you could possibly have any legitimacy.

3.7.2.1 Flexibility

Infrastructure can't ever be really versatile; however, its properties can empower flexible applications running on top of it. A flexible cloud is one that has been outlined such that individual expense of assets, for example, VMs, block storage, and objects are as cheap as could be expected under the circumstances.

Basically, as the relative expense of segments in the framework decreases, applications cannot just expend more, which empowers steering around disappointments, additionally devouring more for the motivations behind scaling application needs here and there, taking into account requests. Generally, you can make the pool bigger and purchase more limits if the individual parts and assets are as shabby as could be expected under the circumstances.

Significant flexible open clouds like Google, Amazon, and Microsoft are giving these sorts of properties, and it's what you have to give inside your four dividers to empower hybridization.

OpenStack will lead you into the future by giving adaptability and execution while supporting versatile applications. Be careful: the OpenStack-fueled cloud working framework that needs you to utilize a fiber channel SAN and blade servers. Those days have gone, as should be obvious with Hadoop.

3.8 Worldwide Backing and Administration Services

Options are you are a worldwide association and want to convey 24x7x365 people to come, cloud-local applications on top of your private, open, and hybrid clouds. You need accomplices who can bolster you universally, who have global experience, and above all who are alright with supporting 24x7x365 situations.

3.8.1   Train Your IT Army to Be the New Cloud Enablers

IT executives are transitioning into cloud overseers. This advancement will be a profound and enduring change inside the undertaking. Altogether new arrangements of abilities should be produced and different aptitudes revived and realigned to the new cloud period. While assessing your OpenStack accomplice, you ought to search for one with huge abilities in preparing, both on nonspecific OpenStack and on their particular cloud working framework item. Above all, while assessing an accomplice who can help you redesign your group's cloud abilities, verify they aren't simply demonstrating how to create on OpenStack or introduce OpenStack. What you truly need is an administrator that is driven, preparing that spotlights on:

- Regular OpenStack structures and particular item designs

- Advantages and disadvantages of different engineering and module/driver decisions

- Versatility, interoperability, and execution issues and choices

- Investigating basic "full stack" issues

- Prologue to how your engineers will utilize your cloud

- Understanding the cloud-local application model

3.8.2   Cloud Bolster Model

Regardless of how great your IT group is, you will require a trusted bolster group to back you up — a group that can bolster your whole framework end-to-end. Verify you ask your Endeavor OpenStack-fueled cloud working framework merchant if their bolster group has upheld high exchange 24x7 situations some time recently. Be sure that they have purported "full stack" bolster capacities. Will they investigate the Linux portion, your hypervisor of decision, systems administration engineering and execution issues, and do they comprehend capacity at a profound level? Clouds are incorporated frameworks and compute, storage, and network administration all touch each other in key ways. Your seller needs to know significantly more than how to design or create for OpenStack. They should be cloud specialists at all levels of the stack. Request it.

3.8.3   Worldwide Service Conveyance

Conveying a cloud universally is no little accomplishment, whether expansive or small. It requires more than simply reach. It requires social affectability and the capacity to comprehend the one of some kind necessities that emerge specifically geologies. For instance, did you realize that while most server farms are more worried over power than space, in Japan it's still normally the exact opposite. Space winds up being one of the single biggest premiums. This space prerequisite is special to their specific surroundings.

Your cloud working framework merchant should have a reputation of effective universal conveyance and an accomplice system that can help with a specific area.

OpenStack is an astonishing, versatile establishment for building a cutting-edge flexible cloud; however it's not great. None of the open source arrangements it contends with are flawless either. Rather, each of these apparatuses is truly a cloud working framework "bit" that can be utilized to convey a more finish, confirmed, Venture-grade cloud working framework (cloudOS). You will require an accomplished endeavor merchant to convey your cloudOS of decision and whether it's OpenStack or another comparative undertaking.

3.9   Mechanization/Automation

Besides, in the initial segment of this book, we secured the part of OpenStack in the up-and-coming era of datacenters. The base has now ended up programmable through APIs. Be that as it may, a huge scale framework utilized by cloud suppliers needs an altogether different methodology keeping in mind the end goal is to set it up with a couple of thousand servers.

For our situation, sending and working the OpenStack Cloud is not as straightforward as you may think. Hence, you require some good times. You have to make any operational undertaking less demanding or, at the end of the day, automated.

3.9.1   DevOps Basically

The term DevOps is a conjunction of development improvement (programming designers) and operations (oversee and place programming into creation). Numerous IT associations have begun to embrace such an idea; however the question is how and what? Is it an occupation? Is it a procedure or a piece of ITIL best practices?

DevOps is a development and operations compound, which essentially characterizes an approach of programming advancement. It depicts hones that streamline the product conveyance process. This is not all. Truth be told, it is more about raising correspondence and combination between developers, administrators (counting executives), and quality certification. The quintessence of the DevOps development is in the advantages of coordinated effort. Diverse controls can identify with DevOps and bring their encounters and abilities together under the DevOps name to assemble a front of shared qualities.

This new development is planned to determine the contention among engineers and administrators. Conveying another discharge influences the creation frameworks that put diverse groups in a change strife. DevOps fills the hole and advances every side core interest.

3.9.2   DevOps and Cloud – Everybody Can Code

How about we cut down the cloud design's layers under the extension and see what we have. Fundamentally, we have SaaS, which works at all layers of the IT stack. At that point comes PaaS, where databases and application compartments are conveyed on interest to achieve the base, where we discover IaaS conveying on-interest assets, for example: VMs, networks, and capacity. Every one of these layers' structures are complete, essential heaps of the cloud. You should consider how every layer of the cloud ought to be created and executed.

Clearly, layered reliance depends on the capacity to make full stacks and convey them under a solicitation of straightforward strides. Keep in mind that we are discussing an extensive versatile environment! The stunning switch to greater situations these days is to disentangle everything however much as can be expected. Framework engineering and programming configuration are turning out to be increasingly confounded. Each new arrival of programming manages new capacities and new arrangements. At that point, you are requested to incorporate the new programming in a specific stage where some way or another, adequate documentation about necessities or investigating is absent! You may ask questions, for example, as to what accomplished something change? What sort of progress? To which individual would it be a good idea for us to relegate a ticket to settle it? Imagine a scenario in which it simply does not work. As indicated by your operational engineers, the product should be overhauled regularly, keeping in mind the end goal to apply the new capacities. The overhaul may happen each time you understand that email requesting that you redesign the product. You may begin to ponder whether your operational engineers will be cheerful about this declaration, in opposition to the product supplier who sent the email with the header, "we are glad to report the arrival of the new form of our product; please push the catch."

We should take a genuine illustration that takes shape this circumstance. An organization's operational group was to a great degree cheerful about buying another capacity machine that functioned admirably on repetition. Amid the initial couple of months, everybody was glad; nothing was broken! It had exactly the intended effect!

At the point when the day came to change the appeal to a genuine cerebral plan, the storage framework neglected to come up short over. Both nodes quit working. Nobody could get to any information! Regardless of the presence of a reinforcement elsewhere, the operational group disliked the "was that HA suitable?" part. In the wake of a monotonous night of examination, the mistake of creating the HA to fall flat was finished up from the log records: there was an apparatus framework upgrade! The past form was by one means or another consequently overhauled and softened the HA capacity up the dynamic node. The redesign was spread to the detached one. Lamentably, the dynamic version chose to fall flat over and tackle the cluster that was passive. In any case, that did not work. It was as though there was a bug some place in the code of the past release!

Shouldn't something be said about on the off chance that you are running comparative answers for different frameworks? Everything is running applications to keep it running! For this situation, it is savvy to stop for some time and make ask questions, for example, this: What is absent? Should I employ more individuals for framework upkeep and investigating? Clearly, on the off chance that you investigate the past case, you will most likely notice that the proprietor of the equipment does not by any stretch of the imagination own it!

The straightforward reason is that being reliant on external gatherings will influence your framework proficiency. All things considered, you may ask a relevant question: should I rework the product apparatus independent from anyone else? How about we reformulate the question: Should I compose the code? The answer, quite often, is yes! It is a questionable answer, isn't that so? How about we continue utilizing case as a part of the request to get out this fogginess. We discussed DevOps, the synergetic point among engineers and operational folks. Everything is conveyed between them on account of the enchantment of DevOps. Keep in mind that it is our objective to disentangle things however much as could be expected! Administrating and sending a huge foundation would not be conceivable without receiving another theory: framework as code. Now, we get another part of the DevOps style: we see our machines as bits of code! Truth be told, we have now appointed the primary errands of DevOps.

Where everything will be seen as code, it may be conceivable to show a given base as modules of code. What you have to do is quite recently theoretical, plan, execute, and send the foundation.

Moreover, in such a worldview, it will be fundamental to stick to the same control as an infrastructure engineer when contrasted with a product designer.

Without uncertainty, these terms are entirely misty at the principal look. Hence, you ought to pose this question identified with our fundamental theme about OpenStack: if infrastructure as code is so vital for a very much sorted out base deployment, what is the situation with OpenStack? The response to this question is moderately straightforward: engineers compute, and network architects and administrators are working close by each other to create OpenStack Cloud that will run our cutting-edge server farm. This is the DevOps soul.

3.9.3   DevOpsifying OpenStack

OpenStack is an open source platform and its code is developed, changed, and altered in each version. Obviously, it is not your essential mission to check the code and plunge into its diverse modules and capacities. This is not our objective! What would we be able to do with DevOps, then? In the long run, we will "DevOps" the code that makes the code run! As you may have seen, a key measure of the accomplishment of a DevOps story is computerization. Everything in a given foundation must be automated!

3.9.3.1 Making the Infrastructure Setup Proficient

At last, the code that digests, models, and assembles the OpenStack infrastructure is resolved to source code administration. In all probability, we achieve a point where we move our OpenStack framework from a code base to a redeployable one by taking after the most recent programming advancement best practices.

At this stage, you ought to know about the nature of your OpenStack infrastructure setup, which generally relies upon the nature of the code that depicts it.

Keeping up the code needs more consideration with a specific end goal to have a sans bug environment when it is conveyed as a last release. We will consider the "bug" term in a foundation development setting as hurtful and practical to the framework.

It is vital to highlight a basic point that you should remember amid all setup stages: automated frameworks are not ready to comprehend human mistake when it is engendered to all bits of your infrastructure. This is vital, and there is no real way to disregard it. The same way is material to the customary programming improvement discipline. You'll need to experience a troupe of stages and cycles utilizing agile approaches to wind up with a last release that is typically a bugless programming form in production.

Keep in mind the illustration given already. Miracles do happen! Be that as it may, if a blunder happens in a little corner of a particular framework and settles in that particular free system, it won't be the same when considering the automation of a substantial base.

3.9.3.2 Conveying OpenStack to the Chain

To keep the OpenStack environment working with a base rate of miracles, guarantee that its infrastructure code conveys the functionalities that are required.

Past these contemplations, we will put the OpenStack arrangement in a toolchain, where it will advise you about how we will direct the base improvement from the test stage to the generation stage. Supporting each apparatus choice must be the reason for your testing tries, and it will likewise help you guarantee that you manufacture the correct thing.

3.9.3.2.1 Constant coordination and conveyance

We should perceive how nonstop incorporation can be connected to OpenStack. Whatever we use for framework administration apparatuses or automation code will be kept as a standard and fundamental topology, as appearing in the following model, where the accompanying necessities are met:

SMTA can be any Framework Administration Apparatus tool, for example, Chef cookbook, puppet modules, Ansible playbook, or juju charms.

VCS stores the past artifacts that are assembled persistently with a ceaseless coordination server. Git can be a decent outfit for our VCS. Then again, you can utilize different frameworks, for example, CVS, Subversion, Bazaar, or whatever other framework that you are most acquainted with.

Jenkins is a flawless instrument that listens to changes in form control and makes the ceaseless mix testing computerized underway clones for test purposes.

The proposed topology for infrastructure as code is comprised of base arrangement configurations (Chef cookbooks, Puppet artifacts, and Vagrant files) that are recorded in a variant control framework and are fabricated consistently by the method for a CI server (Jenkins, for our situation). Base design configuration can be utilized to set up a unit test environment (a virtual domain utilizing Vagrant, for instance) and makes utilization of any framework administration device to procure the base (Chef, Puppet, etc). The CI server continues listening to changes in VCS and naturally proliferates any new forms to be tried, and after that it listens to target situations underway.

Utilizing such model outlines could make our advancement and reconciliation code framework more significant. Clearly, the past OpenStack toolchain highlights the test environment before proceeding onward to creation, which is ordinary! In any case, you ought to give a ton of significance to the testing stage, in spite of the fact that this may be an extremely tedious assignment.

Particular for our situation, with infrastructure code inside OpenStack, things can be troublesome for entangled and ward frameworks. This makes it necessary to guarantee a mechanized and reliable testing of the infrastructure code.

The most ideal approach to do this is to continue testing completely over and over till you are certain about your code. When you are, acquainting changes with your code when it's required shouldn't be an issue.

How about we continue going, get the ideal application running, and push the catch?

3.10   Deploying OpenStack Using Automation

At first sight, you may wonder about the best automation application that will be helpful for our OpenStack "Live day." We have, as of now, picked Git and Jenkins to handle our persistent and conveyance code framework. The time has come to pick the right device for automation.

In the long run, it may be hard to choose the right instrument. No doubt, you'll need to pick between a few of them. Covering all the current IT automation instruments could fill a whole book or even several books. Consequently, giving brief insights on various devices may be useful with a specific end goal to recognize the best toolset for certain specific setups. Obviously, we are still discussing substantial infrastructures with heterogeneous frameworks, a great deal of systems administration, and distributed services.

Giving the chance to one or more apparatuses to be chosen as framework management gatherings can be viable and quick for our arrangement. We will utilize Chef for the following production deployment stage.

On the off chance that you are not acquainted with the Git command line, don't stress; you can utilize an incorporated advancement environment (for example, Eclipse), which gives an extraordinary Git module. Don't hesitate to utilize any Linux conveyance. The following setup will utilize CentOS 6.5 64 bit as the standard working framework.

3.10.1   The Chef and Chef-Based Deployments

When you consider an average Chef, you may consider cookbooks, recipes, and knives! These are what a Chef needs to make great dishes. The essence of the nourishment on a plate relies on upon the innovativeness of the Chef. We do likewise as far as cooking: we utilize an essential cookbook, from which we infer the right formulas. We refine the formulas until we get what satisfies our needs. The server should be up and running.

3.10.1.1   Time to Play with OpenStack Deployment Code

At this stage, we have a complete Chef environment where the OpenStack code foundation will be created, refined, and discharged to generation.

Why don't we investigate the environment topology once more? We require nodes and instances to test how our cookbooks will be connected and tried. For this reason, we will utilize an awesome application tool for testing purposes: **Vagrant**.

Vagrant can be incorporated with Chef. At that point, from a Vagrant record, we push the catch to make Chef run and get nodes up, which makes it the "feline's howl."

There are dependable challenges confronting DevOps, and most likely, they will happen after you have led your outline to be conveyed in a genuine situation. Meeting these difficulties will drive you to obtain new abilities identified with making an extensive confused OpenStack foundation with straightforward code that you never thought you could ace. A few associations and huge organizations have been included in composing cookbooks for OpenStack in various ways. You may be led to think how you can utilize the current cookbooks in the cookbook market and additionally which ones to pick and how to create them for your own needs. Let's examine what we require with the assistance of a straightforward, nonspecific review:

- Controller instances
- Compute instances
- Neutron instances
- Swift as a solitary cluster

You may take note that the controller instance, as depicted in our first outline, handles and runs the dominant part of local OpenStack administrations. You can get numerous formulas from OpenStack cookbooks in GitHub. The Opscode group is additionally an alternative. We will construct our cookbooks in light of StackForge cookbooks. But before that, we should deal with the cookbook dependencies for a clean install and configuration. The common BerkFile for maintaining the dependencies can look like the following:

```
source "https://supermarket.getchef.com"

cookbook 'apache2', '1.9.6'
cookbook 'apt', '2.3.8'
cookbook 'aws', '2.1.1'
cookbook 'build-essential', '1.4.2'
cookbook 'database', '2.2.0'
cookbook 'erlang', '1.4.2'
cookbook 'memcached', '1.7.2'
cookbook 'mysql', '5.4.4'
cookbook 'mysql-chef_gem', '0.0.4'
cookbook 'openssl', '1.1.0'
cookbook 'postgresql', '3.3.4'
cookbook 'python', '1.4.6'
cookbook 'rabbitmq', '3.0.4'
cookbook 'xfs', '1.1.0'
cookbook 'yum', '3.1.4'
cookbook 'selinux', '0.7.2'
cookbook 'yum-epel', '0.3.4'
cookbook 'galera', '0.4.1'
cookbook 'haproxy', '1.6.6'
cookbook 'keepalived', '1.2.0'
cookbook 'statsd', github: 'att-cloud/cookbook-statsd'
cookbook 'openstack-block-storage', github: 'stackforge/cookbook-openstack-block-storage'
cookbook 'openstack-common', github: 'stackforge/cookbook-openstack-common'
cookbook 'openstack-compute', github: 'stackforge/cookbook-openstack-compute'
cookbook 'openstack-dashboard', github: 'stackforge/cookbook-openstack-dashboard'
cookbook 'openstack-identity', github: 'stackforge/cookbook-openstack-identity'
```

```
cookbook 'openstack-image', github: 'stackforge/cookbook-openstack-image'
cookbook 'openstack-network', github: 'stackforge/cookbook-openstack-network'
cookbook 'openstack-object-storage', github: 'stackforge/cookbook-openstack-object-storage'
cookbook 'openstack-ops-database', github: 'stackforge/cookbook-openstack-ops-database'
cookbook 'openstack-ops-messaging', github: 'stackforge/cookbook-openstack-ops-messaging'
```

You can check out the GitHub repositories for OpenStack deployment using chef cookbooks end-to-end flow, so I am not going to add the step-by-step setup of OpenStack. But here I am going to mention the JSON for the role-based deployments.

3.10.1.1.1   os-base.jsons

```
{
  "name": "os-base.json",
  "description": "OpenStack Base Role",
  "json_class": "Chef::Role",
  "default_attributes": {
  },
  "override_attributes": {
  },
  "chef_type": "role",
  "run_list": [
    "recipe[openstack-common]",
    "recipe[openstack-common::logging]",
    "recipe[openstack-common::set_endpoints_by_interface]",
    "recipe[openstack-common::sysctl]"
  ],
  "env_run_lists": {
  }
}
```

3.10.1.1.2   os-compute-worker.json

```
{
  "name": "os-compute-worker",
  "description": "OpenStack Compute Role",
  "json_class": "Chef::Role",
  "default_attributes": {
  },
  "override_attributes": {
  },
  "chef_type": "role",
  "run_list": [
    "role[os-base]",
    "recipe[openstack-compute::compute]"
  ],
  "env_run_lists": {
  }
}
```

3.10.1.1.3   os-base-controller.json

`os-base-controller`

```json
{
  "name": "os-base-controller",
  "description": "OpenStack Controller Role",
  "json_class": "Chef::Role",
  "default_attributes": {
  },
  "override_attributes": {
  },
  "chef_type": "role",
  "run_list": [
    "role[os-base]",
    "role[os-ops-database]",
    "recipe[openstack-ops-database::openstack-db]",
    "role[os-ops-messaging]",
    "role[os-identity]",
    "role[os-image]",
    "role[os-compute-setup]",
    "role[os-compute-conductor]",
    "role[os-compute-scheduler]",
    "role[os-compute-api]",
    "role[os-block-storage]",
    "role[os-compute-cert]",
    "role[os-compute-vncproxy]",
    "role[os-dashboard]"
  ],
  "env_run_lists": {
  }
}
```

The contents of the Vagrant file can like the following:

```ruby
Vagrant.require_version ">= 1.1"

Vagrant.configure("2") do |config|
  # Omnibus plugin configuration
  config.omnibus.chef_version = :latest

  # OpenStack settings
  chef_environment = "vagrant"

    controller_run_list = [
      "role[os-base-controller]",
      "recipe[openstack-network::identity_registration]",
      "role[os-network-openvswitch]",
      "role[os-network-dhcp-agent]",
      "role[os-network-metadata-agent]",
      "role[os-network-server]"
    ]
```

```
  # virtualbox provider settings
  config.vm.provider "virtualbox" do |vb|
    vb.customize ["modifyvm", :id, "--cpus", 4]
    vb.customize ["modifyvm", :id, "--memory", 4096]
    vb.customize ["modifyvm", :id, "--nicpromisc2", "allow-all"]
    vb.customize ["modifyvm", :id, "--nicpromisc3", "allow-all"]
  end

  # OpenStack Controller
  config.vm.define :controller1 do |controller1|
    controller1.vm.hostname = "controller1"
    controller1.vm.box = "opscode-centos-6.5"
    controller1.vm.box_url = "http://opscode-vm-bento.s3.amazonaws.com/vagrant/virtualbox/
opscode_centos-6.5_chef-provisionerless.box"

    controller1.vm.network "forwarded_port", guest: 443, host: 9443     # forward to
dashboard using ssl : dashboard-ssl
    controller1.vm.network "forwarded_port", guest: 8773, host: 9773    # forward to EC2
api : compute-ec2-api
    controller1.vm.network "forwarded_port", guest: 8774, host: 9774    # forward to Compute
API : compute-api
    controller1.vm.network "private_network", ip: "192.168.47.10"
    controller1.vm.network "private_network", ip: "172.16.11.10"

    controller1.vm.provision :chef_client do |chef|
      chef.run_list = controller_run_list
      chef.environment = chef_environment
      # Where to find our Chef Server by providing the authorization key
      chef.chef_server_url = "https://chef.apress.com:443"
      chef.validation_key_path = "/home/apress/chef-repo/.chef/chef-validator.pem"
    end
  end

 # OpenStack Compute

  config.vm.define :compute1 do |apress1|
    compute1.vm.hostname = "apress"
    compute1.vm.box = "opscode-centos-6.5"
    compute1.vm.box_url = "http://opscode-vm-bento.s3.amazonaws.com/vagrant/virtualbox/
opscode_centos-6.5_chef-provisionerless.box"
    compute1.vm.network "private_network", ip: "192.168.19.80"
    compute1.vm.network "private_network", ip: "152.11.24.85"

    compute1.vm.provision :chef_client do |chef|
      chef.run_list = [ "role[os-compute-worker]" ]
      chef.environment = chef_environment
      # Where to find our Chef Server by providing the authorization key
      chef.chef_server_url = "https://chef.apress.com:443"
      chef.validation_key_path = "/home/apress/chef-repo/.chef/chef-validator.pem"
    end
  end
end
```

As you are out there assessing the right merchant to help with your OpenStack appropriation process and the move toward a hybrid cloud, verify how much, if any, of these necessities they can meet. In this section, we secured a few points and wordings on the best way to create and keep up a code infrastructure utilizing the DevOps style.

Conveying your OpenStack framework sending to code won't just rearrange node design or additionally enhance the automation procedure. Despite the fact that we conveyed a fundamental multinode setup of OpenStack in this section, the following part will take you to a third stage, where you can utilize solid methodologies toward augmenting our past outline by clustering, characterizing the cloud controller, and compute hub dispersions.

CHAPTER 4

∎ ∎ ∎

Deploying Multi-Node Cluster

Since you have a lot of great information about the methodologies used to set up a wide OpenStack foundation in an automated way, the time has come to jump farther and cover more particular calculated outlines inside of OpenStack.

In a huge framework, particularly in the event that you are hoping to keep every one of your services up and running, it is vital that you guarantee the OpenStack base is solid and ensures business progression.

We talked about a few outline viewpoints and highlighted some best practices of versatile engineering models inside OpenStack in Chapter 1, "Planning OpenStack Cloud Design Architecture."

We embraced an example design in view of the sample cluster application, and we separated and set up OpenStack services. This is an improved approach to plan a versatile OpenStack environment. Setting up an OpenStack infrastructure in view of the profiled outline, as discussed in the last section, is not straightforward. Despite the fact that we made our outline by dealing with a few viewpoints identified with versatility and execution, we still need to make it genuine. In the event that you are thinking about OpenStack as a solitary block framework, you should step back and recheck what was clarified in a previous section on OpenStack Reference Design.

Before long, we found the enchantment of automation, where we continued an essential setup of one cloud controller together with one compute node utilizing the Chef server.

This chapter starts by covering some clustering angles. It soon enables you to find more OpenStack configuration designs in light of cloud controllers' and process nodes' clustering. Remember that this part won't treat HA as a point of interest and won't touch all OpenStack services layers. Rather, it will target covering a bland diagram of a few potential outcomes of the OpenStack clustering plan. The craft of clustering is the way to giving an answer that fits into a philosophy that hassles institutionalized, steady IT work out OpenStack operations. In this part, we will cover the accompanying points:

- Understanding the craft of clustering

- Characterizing the utilization instance of cloud controllers and compute nodes in an OpenStack domain

- Classifying other OpenStack clustering models in view of cloud controller and compute instance circulation

- Understanding reinforcement systems of cloud controller and compute instances for DR best practices

- Figuring out how to refine your framework code with Chef server for a quick and programmed arrangement

Let's start our journey with understanding clustering for OpenStack design patterns.

Try not to be reluctant to claim that bunching really gives high accessibility in a given foundation. The collection of the limit of two or more servers is intended to be a server clustering. This conglomeration will be performed by a method for the aggregation of a few nodes.

© Uchit Vyas 2016
U. Vyas, *Applied OpenStack Design Patterns*, DOI 10.1007/978-1-4842-2454-0_4

4.1   Hilter Kilter Clustering

Lopsided (Hilter kilter) clustering is for the most part utilized for HA purposes and additionally for the versatility of CRUD operations in databases, informing frameworks, or records.

In such cases, a standby node is included to assume control just if the other node is confronting an occasion of disappointment. We may call the aloof server the languid watcher, where it can incorporate the design of a failover.

4.2   Symmetric Clustering

This is the place all instances are dynamic and a participator handles the procedure of solicitations. This setup may be practical by serving dynamic applications and clients.

A fizzled node can be removed from the cluster, while others assume control over its workload and keep on handling exchanges.

Symmetric clustering can be thought of like a load-adjusting cluster circumstance where all instances share the workload by expanding the execution and adaptability of services running in the cloud-based platform.

4.3   Divide and Rule

OpenStack was intended to be on a level plane versatile; we have now perceived how its services have been broadly appropriated in two ideas: cloud controllers and compute instances.

4.3.1   The OpenStack Cloud Controller

The idea of cloud controllers expects to give one or numerous sorts of focal administration and control over your OpenStack arrangements. We can, for instance, accept that all confirmation and informing exchanges are being overseen by the cloud controller by method for our enchantment center point: the message queue line.

Considering a medium or expansive scale foundation, we will require more than a solitary instance. For an OpenStack cloud administrator, controllers can be considered as an administration aggregator where the dominant part of running services administrations is required for OpenStack to work.

Here is what a cloud controller cloud essentially handles:

- It introduces a principal entryway for access to cloud administration and services utilization.

- It gives the Programming interface administrations so as to convey distinctive OpenStack segments to converse with each other.

- It focuses on an arrangement of exceptionally accessible systems for incorporated administrations by the method for Pacemaker, Corosync, or HAProxy to uncover a VIP for load-adjusting utilities.

- It gives basic framework administrations, for example, database and queue messaging.

- It uncovers the diligent storage, which may be sponsored onto separate storage instances.

We bring, on occasion, the cloud controller as an instance under the extension. This totals the most basic administrations for OpenStack.

4.3.2 Nova-Conductor

On the off chance that you have attempted to introduce OpenStack beginning from the IceHouse or Juno release, while checking Nova administrations running in your OpenStack instance, you may have seen another service called nova-conductor. Try not to freeze! This astounding new service has changed the way the nova-compute administration gets to the database. In the end, it was included for security reasons as compute nodes running the nova-compute services may direct some powerlessness issues. You can envision how assaulting a VM can bring the compute node under the control of the aggressor. Far more detestable, it can bargain the database. At that point, you can figure out the rest: your whole OpenStack cluster setup is under assault! Remember that nova-scheduler is planned to do database operations for the benefit of compute instances.

In this way, you can accept that nova-conductor aggregates another layer on top of nova-compute. Moreover, rather than determining that the multifaceted nature of the database demands bottleneck, nova-conductor parallelizes the solicitations from compute instances.

4.3.3 Nova-Schedular

A few work-process planning studies and executions have been as of late led in distributed computing, by and large keeping in mind the end goal to characterize the best position of asset provisioning. For our situation, we will choose which compute instance will have the VM. It's critical to note that there are clusters of planning calculations in OpenStack. Such inside solicitation data is gotten from the enchantment radio station in the OpenStack center: the message queue.

Nova-scheduler may likewise impact the execution of the hosts running VMs. Along these lines, OpenStack bolsters an arrangement of channels that actualize the accessible instances and gives you the decision to design its choices, taking into account a specific number of measurements and approach contemplations. Furthermore, nova-scheduler can be considered as the leader enclosing a cloud controller instance by applying a couple muddled calculations for the proficient use and situation of VMs. Then again, you ought to comprehend that nova-scheduler accepts a given OpenStack group as a solitary host inside amassed assets of all hosts present in the cluster. This happens when you manage distinctive hypervisors running each of them and their particular planning asset's administration, for example, vCenter inside Dispersed Resource Scheduler (DRS).

In the long run, the scheduler in OpenStack, as you may understand, will keep running in the cloud controller instance. A descent indicates here that necessities be researched: shouldn't something be said about various schedulers in a high accessibility environment? For this situation, we misuse the openness of the OpenStack engineering by running numerous occurrences of every scheduler, as every one of them is listening to the same queue. Know that cinder scheduler is viewed as a scheduling service in OpenStack, which may keep running in the cloud controller instance for block storage administration.

4.3.4 Nova-APIs

More or less, we have officially secured the nova-programming interface administration in Section 1, "Outlining OpenStack Cloud Design." It may be critical to venture forward and discover that nova-programming interface is viewed as the orchestrator engine segment in cloud controller particulars. With no uncertainty, nova-programming interface is gathered in the controller instance in the wake of considering its primary part by tolerating all the approaching Programming interface demands from all segments.

The nova-programming interface service (nova-api) may likewise satisfy more entangled solicitations by passing messages inside different daemons by methods for keeping in touch with the databases and queuing messages. As this service depends on the endpoint idea where all Programming interface queries are started, nova-programming interface gives two diverse APIs utilizing either the OpenStack Programming interface or EC2 Programming interface. This makes it simple to choose which Programming interface will be utilized before conveying a cloud controller instance that may direct to a main problem as you may choose to assume control both APIs. The explanation for this is the heterogeneity of the data presentation utilized by every Programming interface; for instance, OpenStack utilizes names and numbers to allude to occurrence, while the EC2 Programming interface utilizes identifiers like hexadecimal qualities.

Moreover, we have brought compute, identity, image, network, and storage(capacity) APIs to be set in the controller instance, which can likewise be run using other Programming interface administrations. Case in point, we fulfill our arrangement by making an event for the greater part of OpenStack-programming interface service to keep running in the cloud controller instance.

4.3.5 Network Administration

Much the same as OpenStack's Nova administration gives a Programming interface to element solicitations to compute assets, we receive the same idea for the network by permitting its Programming interface to live in the cloud controller, which underpins augmentations to give propelled network abilities: for example, access records and network observing utilizing Neutron. As was accepted in our first model, isolating the majority of the network workers is recommended. Consequently, the cloud controller will incorporate just the Neutron server in the second cycle. Then again, you are enticed to consider the immense measure of movement that hits a cloud controller as to its multirunning administration services; along these lines, you ought to shoulder as a main priority the execution challenges that you may confront. For this situation, clustering best practices come into help your organization become more versatile and expand its execution. The beforehand said methods are crucial, however not adequate. They require essential equipment support with no less than 10 GB of reinforced NICs.

Muddling your execution measurements at such an early stage won't fulfill your topology flexibility. To do as such, versatility elements are dependably there to refine your arrangement. Keep in mind that we tend to scale on a horizontal plane when required.

4.3.6 Image Administration

The cloud controller will likewise be in charge of the conveyance and serving of images utilizing glance programming interface and glance registry, where a choice can be made about which back end will be utilized to dispatch the controller in the cloud.

The glance programming interface underpins a few back-end choices to store images. Swift is a decent option that permits putting away images as objects and gives a versatile arrangement to image storage. Different options are likewise conceivable, for example, filesystem back end and Amazon S3.

4.3.7 The Horizon Choice

As the OpenStack dashboard keeps running in the Apache web server taking into account the Python web application, giving a different instance that can achieve the Programming interface servers in the second step may be an alternative on the off chance that you later choose to diminish the load on your cloud controller instance. A few OpenStack arrangements underway run Horizon in the controller instance yet surrender it over to you to screen it and take separate choices.

4.3.8 Getting Ready for the Message Queue

Unquestionably, you're queuing message framework ought to be grouped. This is another basic subsystem where your instance might be in an end status when the message queue falls flat. We have picked RabbitMQ to handle our queuing framework as it has local grouping support. In any case, it may be excruciating in an expansively scaled OpenStack environment.

A decent practice is to remember such many-sided quality difficulties that must be embraced when we begin a basic cloud controller holding a RabbitMQ administration. It really is great that our configuration is exceptionally flexible and we can group by controller instances; in this manner, we get RabbitMQ clustered. With less controller instances, which require more equipment specs, isolating the RabbitMQ instance bunch will generally be simple.

4.3.9   Controller Consideration

Redundancy is executed by method for virtual IP and Pacemaker. At that point, HAProxy will guarantee load adjusting. Databases and queuing servers have been executed in active/active HA mode when MySQL utilizes Galera for replication, while RabbitMQ is inherently a cluster proficient mode. Different decisions can be made for the present configuration by incorporating, for instance, with Corosync, Pulse, or Keepalived. You can check out the official documentation for further information. When we have recognized which service will be sent in the cloud controller, we hop to the following stride by bringing Chef enthusiastically. We have officially secured a general structure of the OpenStack deployment code using Chef cookbooks, which we have from Chef Store.

As we are going for a scaled framework of OpenStack, we would rather set up the roles and Chef recipes and make them more decoupled for administration instances to achieve a level of high accessibility in the later stage. The cookbook configuration of the cloud controller appears to be much entangled, which suggests that its usage won't not be naturally clear at first look, but rather a brief outline of the cookbooks' connections will make it less demanding for you to highlight the adaptability of this model. Consequently, you may pick up on how to disperse parts and formulas by keeping up the rationale of reliance.

Keeping in our mentality and whatever framework administration instruments we may pick, supporting each service segment on our OpenStack cloud stage must be an adaptable mantra, however much as can reasonably be expected, with the end goal of cloud controller arrangement.

4.3.10   Compute Consideration

Once the orchestrator has assessed the instruments that should be incorporated on the stage, we require the players to perform the tune. The compute instance ought to be independently conveyed in the cluster mode as it structures the assets part of the OpenStack foundation. Indeed, even in another cloud organization design, you may find that the figuring part is for the most part implicit separate ranches. It is necessary to think about the way that compute instance assets should be disregarded in handling, memory, networking, and capacity assets.

From an organization point of view, an OpenStack compute instance won't not be confused to introduce as it will fundamentally run nova-compute and the network agent for Neutron. Be that as it may, its equipment and particular decision won't be self-evident. The cloud controller displays an extensive variety of administrations, yet we have concurred that utilizing HA and a different organization will solidify the cloud controller arrangement. Along these lines, we experience the ill effects of the issue of service downtime. Then again, a compute instance will be the space where the VM will keep running, at the end of the day, the space on which the end client will concentrate on. They just need to push the catch and get the application running on the highest point of your IaaS layer. It is your main goal to ensure an attractive measure of assets.

4.3.11   Overcommitment Contemplations

It would be awesome on the off chance that you could manage the cost of such capable innovation, which is normal these days. Then again, as a rule, the physical compute instances you buy may be more effective than required. To stay away from such misfortune, you ought to remember that estimating your compute instances is imperative.

Nonetheless, this mystical catch-all equation that is pertinent in all cases won't be anything but difficult to discover. You should work through three primary strides:

- Gauge a specimen estimation for the CPU and RAM utilization versus availability.

- Use OpenStack assets' overcommitment without ignoring.

- However much as could be expected, accumulate assets' utilization measurements intermittently.

The craft of memory or CPU measurements is an empowered hypervisor highlight, permitting the utilization of more asset power by the VM than the compute host has. For instance, it permits a host server with 4 GB of physical memory to run 8 VMs, each with 1 GB of memory space assigned.

All things considered, there is no mystery for this situation! You ought to consider the hypervisor; simply figure the segment of physical memory not utilized per VM and dole out it to one that may require more RAM at specific minutes. This is a method based out of the dynamic movement of unused assets that are being held in an unmoving status. Then again, it may be a pleasant component yet without embellishment! It may be risky if assets are depleted and prompt a server crash. Along these lines, we have to plunge into overcommitment use cases.

In OpenStack, you will have the capacity to overcommit CPU and RAM assets by changing as far as possible by their naive arrangement. Compute instances utilize the proportion to decide what number of VMs you can run per equipment thread or center and the amount of memory can be connected with the case. Naturally, OpenStack utilizes 16:1 for CPU designation and 1.5:1 for RAM portion proportions.

4.3.12   Selecting the Virtual Machine Monitor (VMM)

The VMM is the core component of your OpenStack commute instance. This is known as the Hypervisor, which gives an arrangement of sensibility capacities for VMs to get to the equipment layer. The stunning part about hypervisors in OpenStack is the extensive variety of VMMs that it can offer, including KVM, VMware ESXi, QEMU, UML, Xen, Hyper-V, LXC, uncovered metal, and of late, Docker.

The Hypervisor Bolster Lattice (`https://wiki.openstack.org/wiki/HypervisorSupportMatrix`) is a decent reference that can help you to pick what fits your requirements.

OpenStack nova-compute arrangements run KVM as the fundamental hypervisor. The truth of the matter is that KVM is most appropriate for workloads that are locally stateless utilizing `libvirt`. You can look at your compute instance from `/etc/nova/nova.conf` in the accompanying lines:

```
compute_driver=libvirt.LibvirtDriver
libvirt_type=kvm
```

Our further compute setup and deployment will be based out of KVM. While we have chosen to utilize KVM for nova-compute, it is incredible to check how OpenStack could bolster this extensive variety of hypervisors by method for nova-compute drivers. You may be prepared to run your OpenStack surroundings with two or more hypervisors. It can be a client necessity to pick a regular hypervisor keeping in mind the end goal to utilize its local one. In the event that you calculate hypervisors' assortments, don't get confused by the way that a solitary hypervisor is running with an individual compute instance.

4.3.13   RAM and CPU Power Consideration

Shouldn't something be said about shocks? You have done the required asset calculation for your compute instances and need to evaluate what number of virtual machines inside particular flavors can keep running for each that we saw in Chapter 2.

Flavors in OpenStack are an arrangement of equipment layouts that characterize the measure of RAM, disk availability, and the quantity of cores per CPU, etc.

Keep in mind that we just utilize overcommitment when it is required. To make it more profitable, you ought to watch out for your nodes. Remember that gathering asset usage insights is fundamental and will in the long run lead a superior proportion redesign when required. Overcommitting is the beginning stage for execution change of your compute instances; when you consider modifying such a quality, you should know precisely what you require! To answer this question, you will require dynamic checking of the equipment utilization at specific periods. For instance, you may miss a sudden colossal increment in assets' use necessities amid the first or the most recent days of the month for certain client machines, though you were fulfilled by their execution in the center part of the month.

We are discussing top times, which can contrast starting with one physical machine then onto the next. Clients who use virtual cases can't hold the same prerequisites constantly, for instance, financial frameworks. You may confront an exchange off between huge asset assignments to satisfy top times and execution issues while conferring assets. Keep in mind that it is essential to have a solid comprehension of what your framework is virtualizing. Moreover, the more data you assemble, the better arranged and the more prepared you will be to face shocks. Additionally, your central goal is to locate the best enhanced method for taking care of those necessities progressively. At that point, you should pick the privilege hypervisor(s).

4.4 Sample Cluster Deployment

As OpenStack setup full grown from assessment/improvement to creation situations supporting applications and services, or high accessibility, turns into a key prerequisite.

In setup, you would have two controllers, while setting a 3-instance Galera cluster on particular hosts. Presently, it can be a significant jump to run from one VM with all services installed and working on it, to a completely conveyed setup with 5 VMs. The uplifting news is that you can have an HA-based setup beginning with only 3 VMs. Our controllers will run all OpenStack services, and also bunched RabbitMQ and MySQL. A third instance will have a required Galera part (garbd) co-located with a ClusterControl server. The third instance can likewise serve as an OpenStack compute instance.

We will utilize Ubuntu 12.04 LTS 64bit codename on the greater part of our instances. The setup and establishment will be executed as root user, so we expect summon of "sudo - i" order on each SSH session. Make a point to introduce NTP service on all hosts and utilize ntpdate to synchronize from the controller instance NTP daemon. IPtables should be stopped as a matter of course. All instances ought to have two network interfaces, one for Internet while the other one is for OpenStack's intranet utilization. Just the controller instance has a static IP doled out on eth1 while others will remain unconfigured.

Our setup can be represented as shown here.

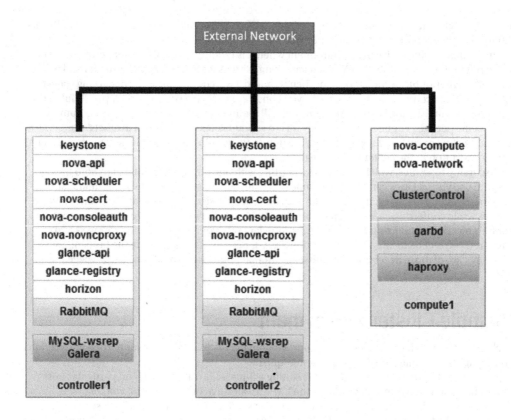

Instances definition arranged in /etc/hosts for each instance will be as shown here:

```
10.1.1.11          controller1
10.1.1.12          controller2
10.1.1.13          compute1 clustercontrol controller mysql
```

4.4.1   Introducing Galera Cluster for MySQL

Galera actualizes a majority-based calculation to choose an essential part through which it upholds consistency. The essential part needs a lion's share of votes, so in a 2-instance framework, there would be no larger part bringing about a split cerebrum. Luckily, it is conceivable to include a garbd (Galera Daemon), which is a lightweight stateless daemon that can go about as the odd instance. Arbitrator disappointment does not influence the cluster operations and another occasion can be reattached to the cluster whenever. There can be a few authorities in the cluster.

ClusterControl has support for conveying garbd on non-database instances. The Galera Configurator more often than not needs no less than four instances for a 3+1 bootstrapping and configuration. Once the deployment and setup is done for Galera cluster, ensure that two masters with a garbd instance show up in the ClusterControl rundown bar:

■ **Database Clusters**

● **default_name** GALERA [ACTIVE]   Cluster ID: 1   Queries: 2/s   CONNECTIONS: 20   Controller: ✔   MASTER: ✔ ✔   GARBD: ✔

🔲 Overview   🎲 Nodes   📊 Query Monitor   📈 Performance 0   💾 Backup 0   🔧 Manage   👥 Alarms 0   📑 Logs 10   🔧

4.4.2   Setting Up HAproxy

We will setup HAproxy to load parity MySQL Galera cluster and other OpenStack segments. By clicking on the "Add Load Balancer" button from the ClusterControl dashboard, you will be able to set up the compute1 instance as the load balancer.

Right now, HAproxy loadbalances MySQL asks for on port 33306 on the ClusterControl instance. So to change the setup, include taking after lines into /etc/haproxy/haproxy.cfg:

```
listen glance_api_cluster
        bind *:9292
        balance  source
        option  tcpka
        option  httpchk
        option  tcplog
        server controller1 10.1.1.11:9292 check inter 2000 rise 2 fall 5
        server controller2 10.1.1.12:9292 check inter 2000 rise 2 fall 5
listen glance_registry_cluster
        bind *:9191
        balance  source
        option  tcpka
        option  tcplog
        server controller1 192.168.1.11:9191 check inter 2000 rise 2 fall 5
        server controller2 192.168.1.12:9191 check inter 2000 rise 2 fall 5
listen keystone_admin_cluster
        bind *:35357
        balance  source
        option  tcpka
        option  httpchk
        option  tcplog
        server controller1 10.1.1.11:35357 check inter 2000 rise 2 fall 5
        server controller2 10.1.1.12:35357 check inter 2000 rise 2 fall 5
listen keystone_public_internal_cluster
        bind *:5000
        balance  source
        option  tcpka
        option  httpchk
        option  tcplog
        server controller1 10.1.1.11:5000 check inter 2000 rise 2 fall 5
        server controller2 10.1.1.12:5000 check inter 2000 rise 2 fall 5
listen nova_ec2_api_cluster
        bind *:8773
        balance  source
        option  tcpka
        option  tcplog
```

```
        server controller1 10.1.1.11:8773 check inter 2000 rise 2 fall 5
        server controller2 10.1.1.12:8773 check inter 2000 rise 2 fall 5
listen nova_compute_api_cluster
        bind *:8774
        balance source
        option   tcpka
        option   httpchk
        option   tcplog
        server controller1 10.1.1.11:8774 check inter 2000 rise 2 fall 5
        server controller2 10.1.1.12:8774 check inter 2000 rise 2 fall 5
listen nova_metadata_api_cluster
        bind *:8775
        balance source
        option   tcpka
        option   tcplog
        server controller1 10.1.1.11:8775 check inter 2000 rise 2 fall 5
        server controller2 10.1.1.12:8775 check inter 2000 rise 2 fall 5
```

Once done, restart the HAproxy service. For further installation of OpenStack components, you can follow standard OpenStack installation method or the automated way using Chef cookbooks. So as per mentioned IP address for the machines, sample nova.conf will likely be following the some way on both controllers:

```
[DEFAULT]
...
my_ip=192.168.210.21
vncserver_listen=0.0.0.0
vncserver_proxyclient_address=10.1.1.21
glance_host=controller
network_manager=nova.network.manager.FlatDHCPManager
firewall_driver=nova.virt.libvirt.firewall.IptablesFirewallDriver
network_size=254
allow_same_net_traffic=False
multi_host=True
send_arp_for_ha=True
share_dhcp_address=True
force_dhcp_release=True
flat_network_bridge=br100
flat_interface=eth1
public_interface=eth1
rabbit_hosts = controller1:5672,controller2:5672
rabbit_retry_interval = 1
rabbit_retry_backoff = 2
rabbit_max_retries = 0
rabbit_durable_queues = False
rabbit_ha_queues = True
rabbit_password = guest
auth_strategy = keystone
irpc_backend = nova.rpc.impl_kombu
[database]
connection = mysql://nova:yournovapassword@mysql:33306/nova
```

Once Nova, Horizon, Keystone, and RabbitMQ setup and configurations are done, you will be able to see the following OpenStack dashboard at `http://10.1.1.11/horizon`.

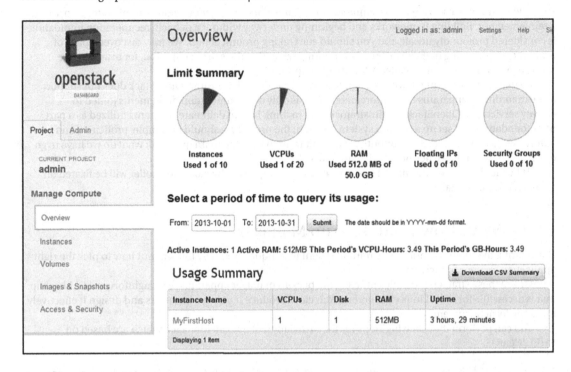

Try to log in into ClusterControl at `http://10.1.1.21/clustercontrol` to check your Galera Cluster information about nodes and other details.

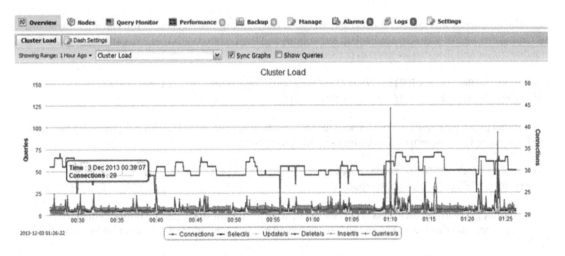

This is just a sample cluster deployment and management but we have not covered Glance component.

4.5   Everything Can Be Failed

A standout among the most basic assignments for a framework manager or cloud administrator is to arrange a reinforcement. Building frameworks and beginning underway without a debacle recuperation foundation is considered profoundly unsafe and you should start taking prompt action. We may discover a pack of property programming in the distributed computing range that does the occupation, for example, the VMware backup arrangement called VMware Backup solution.

Be that as it may, going down open source clouds won't be that simple. OpenStack does not support any extraordinary apparatus for reinforcement. As it is only an accumulation of segments joined to convey services, an OpenStack administrator ought to think how to delineate segments utilized as a part of its foundation and set up a backup system for each; the procedure should be simple, proficient, and autorecovery empowered. Subsequently, you don't want to miss the main question: what do we have to go down and how would we perform such a mission?

At first look, you may be enticed to surmise that moving down the cloud controller will be fixated on setup records and databases.

4.5.1   Move Down with Backup Manager

Considering that there are numerous reinforcement techniques, you may think about how to pick the right application for your framework.

One of these strategies includes utilizing the backup manager apparatus: a straightforward CLI backup that is accessible for most Linux circulations. You can introduce it on your instances and design it effectively from one focal document.

You can perform the following steps for the installation of Backup Manager, which are based on RHEL/CentOS.

```
$ sudo rpm -Uvh http://mirrors.kernel.org/fedora-epel/6/i386/epel-release-6-8.noarch.rpm
$ sudo rpm --import /etc/pki/rpm-gpg/RPM-GPG-KEY-EPEL-6
$ sudo yum install backup-manager
```

The primary design record for backup manager is /etc/backup-manager.conf. You can alter the record by characterizing every area by the backup techniques and their related variables. We can begin by posting the directories and files that we need to consider as backup:

```
export BM_TARBALL_DIRECTORIES="/var/lib/nova /etc/keystone  /etc/cinder /etc/glance /var/
lib/glance /var/lib/glance/images  /etc/mysql"
```

At that point, we determine the backup techniques, for example, mysql utilizing mysqldump and tarball to characterize the rundown of directories of relating tarballs:

```
export BM_ARCHIVE_METHOD="tarball mysql"
export BM_REPOSITORY_ROOT="/var/backups/"
```

You may get ready for an excess arrangement by transferring the documented reinforcement to an auxiliary server utilizing rsync. You can utilize your Swift group to give more information excess over the Swift rings.

The drawback of this methodology is the plain text presentation of the secret word of databases. In this manner, on the off chance that you mean to secure the database, guarantee that the authorizations are confined /etc/backup-manager.conf, including the root user.

Shouldn't something be said about compute nodes? Truth be told, it infers the same envelope, /var/lib/nova/, and rejects the subdirectory examples where the live KVM dwells. Going down the occasions themselves is likewise conceivable by either making a preview from Horizon or by introducing a backup device in the occurrence itself.

In this part, you figured out how to circulate services among cloud controllers by taking future setups in light of central ideas about HA and services clustering into thought. You additionally figured out how a cloud controller is formed and about its capacities in an OpenStack cloud platform setup. By separating the cookbooks, we transferred on Chef server, and you secured an illustration that indicated how you could play with parts to characterize your own services for them to be reusable with different formulas. You should likewise have taken in the significance of compute instance prerequisite from an equipment point of view by refining the choice identified with hypervisor determination and how to lead the best storage outfit for your compute instance.

Another critical point was highlighted, which examines how to move down your OpenStack surroundings. This is not something to overlook; as your OpenStack establishment develops, the span of plate use per instance may increment drastically and can cut it down effectively. For this situation, we need to look at the capacity approaches existing in OpenStack and how to tackle them to be helpful for various purposes.

CHAPTER 5

■ ■ ■

Nova Architecture and Deployment

Nova OpenStack Compute service is utilized for facilitating and overseeing distributed computing frameworks. It is a part-based engineering empowering snappier increases of new components. It is disaster tolerant, recoverable, and gives Programming interface similar frameworks like Amazon Elastic Compute Cloud(EC2).

Nova is based on an informed engineering and the greater part of its segments can usually be keep running on a few servers. This design permits the segments to convey through a message line. Conceded articles are utilized to abstain from blocking while a part sits tight in the message queue for a reaction.

Nova, together with its segments, share a brought together SQL-based database. This is appropriate for smaller setups. However, for bigger arrangements a conglomeration framework will be set up to deal with the information over different information stores.

5.1   Nova Design Engineering

Nova is architected as a distributed application with numerous segments, yet most of these are custom-composed Python daemons of two assortments:

- Web Server Gateway Interface (WSGI)* applications to get and intervene Programming interface calls

- Worker daemons to complete orchestration errands

Notwithstanding, there are two fundamental bits of the design that are neither custom composed nor Python-based: the messaging queue and the database. These two segments encourage the nonconcurrent coordination of complex errands through message passing and data sharing. See Figure 5-1.

© Uchit Vyas 2016

U. Vyas, *Applied OpenStack Design Patterns*, DOI 10.1007/978-1-4842-2454-0_5

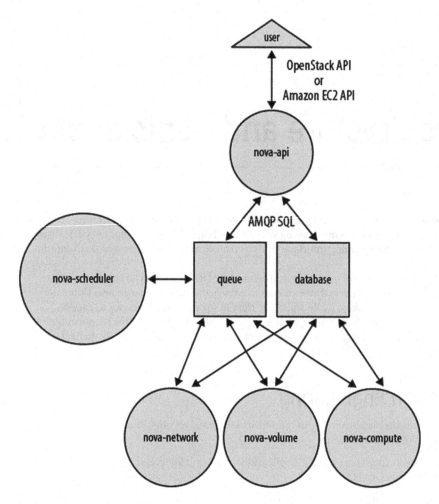

Figure 5-1. *Nova consistent design*

This confounded outline can be summed up in three sentences:

- End clients who need to utilize Nova to make compute nodes call nova-programming interface with OpenStack Programming interface or EC2 Programming interface demands.

- Nova daemons trade data through the queue (activities) and database (data) to complete Programming interface demands.

- Glance is a totally isolated service that Nova interfaces via the Glance Programming interface to give virtual disk imaging administrations.

Now that we've seen the diagram of the procedures and their communications, let's investigate every segment.

5.1.1   Nova-API

The nova-api interface daemon is the core part of Nova engineering stack. You may see it outlined on numerous photos of Nova as Programming interface and "Cloud Controller." While this is mostly valid, cloud controller is truly only a class (particularly the CloudController in nova/api/ec2/cloud.py) inside the nova-programming interface daemon. Its main role is to acknowledge and satisfy approaching Programming interface demands.

To acknowledge and satisfy Programming interface demands, nova-api gives an endpoint to all Programming interface inquiries (tolerating demands utilizing either the OpenStack Programming interface or the Amazon EC2 Programming interface), starts a large portion of the coordination exercises (for example, running an occurrence), and implements some approach (for the most part quota checks). For a few solicitations, it will satisfy the whole demand itself by questioning the database and afterward giving back the answer. For more muddled solicitations, it will pass messages to different daemons through a mix of composing data to the database and adding messages to the queue.

As a matter of course, nova-programming interface listens on port 8773 for the EC2 Programming Interface and 8774 for the OpenStack Programming interface.

5.1.2   Nova-Scheduler

The nova-scheduler procedure is theoretically the most straightforward bit of code in Nova: it takes a VM occasion demand from the queue and figures out where it ought to run (particularly, which register server host it should keep running on). Be that as it may, this will develop to be the most complex piece, as it needs to calculate the present condition of the whole cloud foundation and apply complex calculations to guarantee productive utilization. With that in mind, nova-scheduler executes a pluggable design that gives you a chance to pick (or compose) your own technique for planning and scheduling. Table 5-1 shows the different schedulers and decisions.

Table 5-1. *Nova Schedulers*

Scheduler	Description
Straightforward	Endeavors to discover slightest stacked host.
Chance	Picks arbitrary accessible host from administration table. This is the default scheduler.
Zone	Picks arbitrary host from inside an accessibility zone.

To represent how basic nova-scheduler can be, here is the significant code from the chance scheduler class in nova/schedule/chance.py:

```
class ChanceScheduler(driver.Scheduler):
"""Implements Scheduler as a random host selector."""
def schedule(self, context, topic, *_args, **_kwargs): """Picks a node that is up at random."""
hosts = self.hosts_up(context, topic) if not hosts:
raise driver.NoValidHost(_("Scheduler was unable to locate a host" " for this request. Is
the appropriate"
" service running?")) return hosts[int(random.random() * len(hosts))]
```

As should be obvious from the above code instance, the timetable strategy basically picks a random host from the variety of hosts that are as of now known as "up and running."

5.1.3   Compute Worker Daemon

The nova-compute procedure is essentially a worker daemon that makes and ends VM nodes. The procedure by which it does as such is genuinely perplexing, yet the nuts and bolts are straightforward: acknowledge activities from the queue; and after that perform one or a progression of VM Programming interface gets to do them while overhauling state in the database. A case of this would be nova-compute tolerating a message from the queue to make another occasion and after that utilizing the libvirt library to begin another KVM node.

There is an assortment of ways that nova-compute oversees VMs. The most widely recognized is through a product bundle called libvirt. This is a toolbox (Programming interface, daemon, and utilities) made by Red Hat to collaborate with the capacities of an extensive variety of Linux virtualization advances. While libvirt might be the most widely recognized, nova-compute additionally utilizes the Xen Programming interface, vSphere Programming interface, Windows Administration Interface, and others to bolster other virtualization innovations. One of the qualities of Nova is its wide backing for virtualization advancements. The virtualization innovations bolstered in the present release form of Nova are taken point by point in Table 5-2 below.

Table 5-2. *Virtualization Support in Nova*

Virtualization Item	upheld	interface	Bolster description
KVM	Yes	libvirt	Most famous innovation for mid-scale arrangements. Apparently the least demanding to set up and design. Underpins propelled operations, for example, live migration and resize.
Xen	Yes	libvirt	Most well-known (alongside XCP/XenServer) innovation for bigger scale and deployment arrangements.
Citrix Xen-Server	Yes	XenAPI	Citrix's business form of Xen-based virtualization item. Underpins propelled highlights.
XCP	Yes	XenAPI	The open source form of Citrix XenServer accessible under the LGPL, GPL, Q Public License v1. Bolsters subset of XenServer elements.
ESX/ESXi	Yes	vSphere API	Most well-known enterprise class virtualization platform.
VSphere	No	VSphere API	
User Mode Linux	Yes	libvirt	For the most part considered a lower execution virtualization choice, UML runs every visitor as a customary procedure in client space.
Hyper-V	Yes	WMI	Hyper-V is Microsoft's virtualization innovation.
QEMU	Yes	libvirt	Gives the premise to most Linux-based virtualization advancements, (for example, KVM and VirtualBox).
LXC (Supported in Kilo release)	Yes	libvirt	LXC is a working OS framework level apportioning innovation that takes into consideration running different secluded servers (compartments) in a solitary kernel. LXC does not really virtualize the server. Rather, it furnishes a virtual domain with its own particular procedure space. While this doesn't give the same level of disengagement (as each segment shares the normal piece of kernel), it might give a few points of interest in I/O execution.
VirtualBox	No		

5.1.4 Volume Worker Daemon

As you can assemble by the name, nova-volume deals with the creation, joining, and separating of steady volumes to register nodes. It can utilize volumes from an assortment of suppliers, for example, iSCSI or AoE. Table 5-3 demonstrates the present volume supplier alternatives.

Table 5-3. *Nova Volume Supplier choices*

Volume supplier	Description
iSCSI	A normally utilized IP-based exemplification of SCSI command-line arguments. This is bolstered by the most cutting-edge working OS frameworks, yet the Nova usage just as of now backs Linux with this execution. This driver supports CHAP for validation.
AoE	Superior layer 2 Ethernet innovation that epitomizes SATA command-line arguments in Ethernet outlines. Bolstered on Linux through the AoE Tools bundle, particularly the vblade program.
sheepdog	An open source, disseminated storage framework particularly intended for QEMU/KVM establishments that is produced by NTT Laboratories.
Solaris iSCSI	Bolsters Solaris-facilitated iSCSI volumes and utilizations ZFS summons.
RBD	RADOS block device (RBD) driver to communicate with Ceph, a disseminated document framework taking into account a dependable and versatile conveyed object store.
LeftHand	A driver for interfacing with HP Lefthand SAN arrangements (starting now known as "HP P4000 SAN Solutions"). Dissimilar to different suppliers specified over, this supplier does not run specifically on the SAN equipment. Rather, it gets to it by means of SSH command-line arguments.

5.1.5 Network Worker Domain

The nova-network worker daemon is fundamentally the same as nova-compute and nova-volume. It acknowledges organizing assignments from the queue and after that performs framework command-line arguments to control the system.

Nova characterizes two unique sorts of IP locations : for example, Fixed IPs and Floating IPs. These can be extensively considered as private IPs (fixed) and open IPs (floating). Fixed IPs are appointed on host startup and continue as before during their whole lifetimes. Floating IPs are progressively allotted and related to an area permitted outside the network.

To bolster the task and availability of fixed IPs, Nova underpins three networking administrators:

- Flat is the most fundamental system director. Each new occurrence is allotted a fixed IP and appended to a typical extension (which must be made by the administrator). IP design data must be "infused" (built into the new node virtual disk image) to arrange the host.

- FlatDHCP expands upon the Flat administrator by giving DHCP administrations to handle host tending to and formation of extensions.

- VLAN underpins that generally highlight. In this mode, nova-network makes a VLAN, a subnet, and a different extension for every undertaking. Every undertaking additionally gets a scope of IP just available inside the VLAN.

Of these three system chiefs, VLAN is the most highlighted, Flat is the most frills (however adaptable), and FlatDHCP strikes a pleasant harmony between the two.

5.1.6   Queue

The queue gives a focal center point to passing messages between daemons. This is right now executed with RabbitMQ, yet hypothetically could be any AMPQ message queue upheld by the Python ampqlib and carrot libraries.

Nova makes a few sorts of message queues to encourage correspondence between the different daemons. These include themes queues, fanout queues, and host queues. Themes queues permit messages to be communicated to the quantity of specific class of worker daemons. For instance, Nova utilizes these to pass messages to all (or any) of the compute or volume daemons. This permits Nova to utilize the most readily accessible worker to prepare the message. Host queues permit Nova to send messages to particular administrations on particular hosts. For instance, Nova regularly needs to make an impression on a particular host's compute worker to make a move on a specific occasion. Fanout queues are just presently utilized for the promoting of the administration capacities to nova-scheduler workers.

Here is a case of the queues made in RabbitMQ for a straightforward, holding-nothing-back one-node establishment:

```
$ sudo rabbitmqctl list_queues
Listing queues ... scheduler_fanout_15a3251f5ac34aae49785743911e9837 0 volume 0 volume_
fanout_e57538edafb84ab8aad8d85e43781237 0 compute_fanout_38a37d3dc7564b66a5a540a1e222b1
2b 0 compute.cactus 0 volume_fanout_d62eb016a948573f5583c34d5a5fbb0a5 0 volume_fanout_
abdbab4bde30164ff8b84439041e31052 0 volume.cactus 0 network_fanout_42a6ba59c3b25d6b9ca69413
8b652152 0 compute 0 network_fanout_256426267c5b745b5a2ba117bc5abe5c 0 compute_fanout_85234b
b09b8a3b2ab3552bbe87a52c44 0 scheduler 0
network.cactus 0
network 0 scheduler_fanout_5111c5b6e6d3475a7c424ff5eba33b0d 0 scheduler.cactus 0
```

5.1.7   Database

As expressed before, Nova utilizes a Python library called SQL-Alchemy for database reflection and access. Thus, Nova can hypothetically bolster any database item that SQL-Alchemy underpins. Nonetheless, practically speaking, there are just three with any level of testing and backing inside the Nova people group:

- sqlite3

- While sqlite3 is the default database for improvement and testing, it is inadmissible for live deployments at production environments because of versatility, accessibility, and execution concerns.

- MySQL

  MySQL is by a long shot the most prevalent database for Nova production configuration and deployments. It is additionally seemingly most straightforward to set up with Nova, and the majority of the documentation expects you are utilizing it. It should be the default decision for clients.

- PostgreSQL

- PostgreSQL is a far-off third in use inside the Nova people group. In any case, there is a devoted gathering utilizing it and it possesses numerous favorable components for use in expansive scale creation destinations. Clients with solid involvement in conveying and tuning PostgreSQL may discover this is an alluring choice.

Let's assume that you are searching for a production configuration-based deployment, the choice for a database item ought to come down to PostgreSQL or MySQL. Unless you have huge involvement with PostgreSQL, MySQL will be a superior decision, as all documentation is composed because of MySQL and there is a bigger bolster group.

The database stores a large portion of the arrangement and runtime state for some cloud environments. This incorporates the occurrence sorts that are accessible for use, occasions being used, accessible networks, and ventures.

Table 5-4. *Some of the Nova db schema*

Table Detail	Notes
compute_nodes	Abilities (vcpus, memory, and so on.) and state (vcpus utilized, memory utilized, and so on.) of each register instance.
networks	Data relating to networks characterized in Nova. Incorporates IP to, VLAN, and VPN data.
auth_tokens	Maps Authorization tokens (for all API exchanges) to genuine clients.
projects	Data about projects, including venture chief.
instances	Description of VM nodes.
key_pairs	Key-pair for ssh connection.
instance_types	Details (vCPUs, RAM, and so forth.) of flavors or nodes sorts that clients can use in this cloud.
instance_metadata	Metadata key/value sets for the node that is utilized amid node startup.
instance_actions	Records visitor VM's activities and results.
auth_tokens	Maps tokens (for all Programming interface exchanges) to genuine clients
consoles	Console session for the node.
export_devices	Rack and blade data utilized fundamentally with the AoE volume driver.
certifiates	Mappings for client, ventures, and x509 declarations records.
console_pools	Pool of consoles on the similar static node.
migrations	Utilized for running host-to-host movement.
Migrate_version	Stores current form of the database schema and in addition other movement-related data. Just utilized inside and by engineers amid redesigns.

5.2   Nova Deployment Phases

As Nova backs an extensive variety of advancements, arrangements, and outlines, it will be imperative to make various engineering and plan choices before hoping to send it. This area guides you through the most vital ones before you start. Setup of Nova can be easy with great arranging. Be that as it may, Nova has a great deal of moving parts, so it's great to comprehend a review of what it takes to be proficient before you begin introducing application.

This is a three-stage procedure:

- Arranging Nova setup to settle on deployment situation, conclude key configuration decisions, and guarantee equipment meets necessities.

- Introducing Nova to get the product, requirements, and designs onto the instances.
- Utilizing Nova to prep the framework for your underlying clients.

At every period of the setup, we will make a point to test the after effects of our activities. See Figure 5-2.

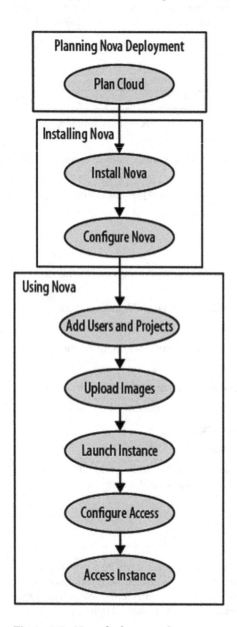

Figure 5-2. *Nova deployment phases*

Without these tests, it is anything but difficult to get to the last stride and discover you have to begin once again because of a blunder in an early stage.

5.2.1   Virtualization Innovation

As should be obvious from the prior dialog of Nova's design, there are plentiful decisions for virtualization items. I won't go into every one of the components about the fitting virtualization innovation to pick here, yet in the event that you have an introduced a base of hypervisors, this should be figured into your cloud stage decision.

Unless you as of now have broad involvement with specific virtualization innovation, a great many people will incline toward either KVM or a Xen-based arrangement (Xen/XCP). Each has its own particular points of interest:

- KVM comes up with most working OS frameworks and is simple to set up and design. It has seemingly the best backing inside Nova (supporting propelled Nova highlights like live movement) and is anything but difficult to get support on, as it is utilized generally as a part of the group. Nonetheless, numerous individuals feel that it has more prominent overhead (particularly in I/O) and doesn't bolster some top-of-the line virtualization like memory ballooning.

- Xen-based arrangements, then again, exceed expectations at execution and have been utilized as a part of a portion of the biggest clouds on the planet. It is supposed to power Rackspace's cloud, Amazon's EC2, and GoGrid's cloud. Be that as it may, this comes at the cost of unpredictability, as they are significantly more difficult to introduce, design, and keep up for individuals unpracticed with big business virtualization items.

The general dependable guideline at the present time is to arrange KVM for little or non-active deployable organizations yet utilize a Xen-based innovation for vast scale generation establishments.

5.2.2   Authentication

Nova can validate against various sources. Of course, it will utilize the nearby setup database (the one indicated by the - sql_connection banner) for this. Be that as it may, the present form of Nova likewise bolsters LDAP for validation. LDAP validation requires fundamentally more setup. Setup help is accessible for OpenSSH, OpenLDAP, Sun's LDAP, and OpenDJ. For more data about setting up these choices, counsel the nova/auth/ in the Nova source.

5.2.3   Scheduler

There are numerous decisions for your scheduler. As expressed before, this is an adroit basic, however fundamentally vital piece of your design and setup. The scheduler places nodes (VMs) onto particular compute instances. While this may not be essentially vital on the off chance that you just have maybe a couple compute nodes, it is totally basic once you begin to develop. Most establishments will begin with the straightforward scheduler and after that compose their own scheduler as they develop. In the event that written work on your own scheduler is not doable for your establishment, the following form of Nova will highlight more decisions.

5.2.4   API

Nova includes a pluggable design for Programming interface support. The present Nova incarnation underpins:

- OpenStack API
- Amazon EC2 API

Numerous clients will presumably ask for the for the most part perfect EC2 Programming interface, which bolsters around 90% of Amazon's present execution. Be that as it may, the OpenStack Programming interface will most likely be the all the more broadly actualized version over the long haul, as it is an open Programming interface not controlled by a solitary organization.

While there is no specialized necessity to pick one Programming interface over the other, it will be optional to your clients on the off chance that they have to utilize both. Not many clients' instruments or libraries will bolster both and permit them to switch on a Programming interface by a Programming interface call premise.

5.2.5   Volumes

Volume storage configuration should be treated with specific consideration, as it is one of only a handful couple of parts of Nova that stores as non-fleeting information. Most vast establishments will take a chance at utilizing either the SAN or iSCSI choices for this, as it permits them to use undertaking class equipment and programming for more prominent accessibility and repetition. Be that as it may, specialized establishments (particularly elite processing or research) may attempt the less creation prepared drivers (RDB or Sheepdog) if their information survivability is not standard sum.

5.2.6   Image Administration

Images can be an administration pain for some establishments. While utilizing Look alongside Glance is the reasonable decision for bigger establishments, its administration overhead and extra arrangements for quality might be a lot for smaller organizations. In these cases, nova-objectstore is likely the best option.

5.3   Setting Up Nova

With the nuts and bolts and hypothesis behind us, the time has come to deep dive with Nova and introduce the code on a server. In this part, we will stroll through the setup and configuration overview of Nova on a solitary node with both the StackOps distro and Ubuntu bundles. You'll get an inclination for the complexities of executing your configuration decisions in genuine use. While these establishments will be just single nodes, they will contain the whole exhibit of OpenStack programming and elements.

5.3.1   Nova with StackOps

StackOps gives a distro to OpenStack supported with a bare-metal installer. The bare-metal installer robotizes the vast majority of the setup and configuration errands, leaving next to no cli or setup record altering for the head. It will introduce a working OS framework, fundamental programming bundles, and Nova setup documents for us. One can go with DevStack setup also instead of StackOps.

5.3.2   Align with StackOps Requirements and Installations

While insignificant prerequisites will get the framework introduced and running, you will be obliged in the quantity of VMs that you can dispatch. At the base 2GB of RAM, you may just have the capacity to dispatch a solitary little node. Negligible setup ought to have the capacity to be fulfilled by most systems or servers purchased inside the most recent couple of years.

Obviously, the insignificant necessities are helpful for a proof of idea or development framework, yet it fits consummately for some requirements. An all the more fittingly arranged framework could be utilized as a deployable productive framework. The gauge for this would be as appeared in Table 5-5.

Table 5-5. *System Particulars for StackOps*

Segment	Particular
CPU	2 x Intel/AMD x64
RAM	32 GM (min)
Disk	2 x 2TB SATA RAID 1 Drives
	2 x 32GB SAS/SSD/SATA RAID 1 Drives
NIC	2 x 1GbE

Once you will have the StackOps source available with you and attached as USB or CD, you will be able to see following screen as shown in Figure 5-3.

Figure 5-3. *StackOps installation screen*

In the wake of picking the "Install StackOps Controller Node," you'll be driven through various standard Linux establishment screens. They will get some information about your dialect and console design before introducing various essential segments.

After it has finished the fundamental segments establishment, it will request that you design your system settings. Enter your IP address, network IP, netmask, and default gateway address. It will then attempt and contact an open NTP server. On the off chance that it falls flat, it will request that you determine one with your efforts.

5.3.2.1 Set Up with Smart Installer

With the essential distro effectively introduced, it is presently time to design the Nova delicate product. StackOps has an agent-based "Smart Installer" that aides you through the design and configuration process, gives you clever defaults, and after that applies the arrangement to your recently introduced server. While we are just utilizing it for a straightforward stand-alone instance here, it will likewise design and apply to different servers as per their part in the sending situation.

The initial phase in running the Smart Installer is to interface a web program as `http://xxx.xxx.xxx.xxx:8888`, where xxx.xxx.xxx.xxx is your server's IP. When you associate with that location, you will be diverted to Smart Installer login screen as seen in Figure 5-4.

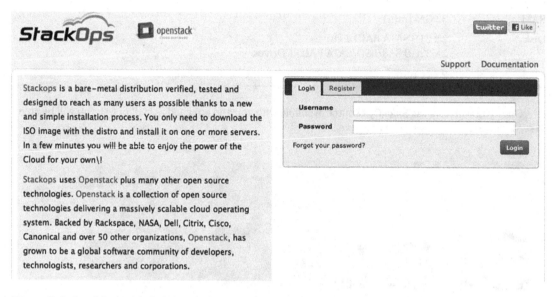

Figure 5-4. *StackOps Login Screen*

Once enlisted and signed in, the Smart Installer will step you through various screens to arrange your Nova organization. The main screen is the most vital: choosing your deployment scenario. See Figure 5-5.

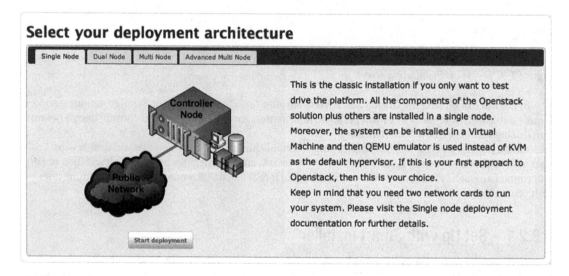

Figure 5-5. *StackOps Single Node*

Next, it will help you design your controller capacities (nova-programming interface, networks, information base, queue, and so forth) of your establishment.

When you survey the equipment setups, you can progress to the product necessities screen. This is likewise a read-just screen, and subsequent to checking on your server network setup, you can go ahead to the following screen. The following screen demonstrates the design alternatives for system topologies. Since we are utilizing a solitary interface demo server, we don't have to change anything (it ought to be preset to your eth0 interface). In more propelled sending situations, this screen gives you a chance to appoint separate service, storage, and network systems. Go ahead to the following screen.

When you are fulfilled by your system alternatives, proceed onward to the process screen. The main alternative that you might need to audit is your libvirt sort. This draw-down menu gives you a chance to pick among QEMU and KVM virtualization. Unless you don't have a KVM enabled system, you ought to abandon it on KVM.

The last arrangement screen for the Smart Installer is the volume choices. You may need to change the lvm_device alternative to the gadget way for your unfilled allotment that you made. With the volume arrangement done, you are prepared to introduce your setup to your server, as Figure 5-6 shows.

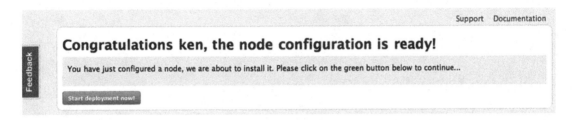

Figure 5-6. *StackOps Configuration Success Screen*

Since we have completed the setup and configuration of the system, how about we ensure that everything is up and running. Sign into your Nova server as root with the "stackops" secret password. Once you've signed into the server, add the Nova binaries to your PATH.

```
# export PATH=$PATH:/var/lib/nova/bin/
```

At that point check to ensure every one of the administrations are up and running with the "nova-manage" command from CLI.

Another way that you can go ahead with package installation is with standard installation steps available over the Web in multiple places.

CHAPTER 6

■ ■ ■

Exploring through Neutron

Undertakings, both substantial and small, run their clouds utilizing OpenStack programming. While the clouds themselves may differ in unpredictability, one thing is consistent: they are made conceivable by the adaptability and adaptability of OpenStack Compute and Networking administrations. The Neutron venture code name is generally utilized as a part of the OpenStack people group to portray the SDN method of OpenStack Networking and was known before as Quantum; yet because of copyright reasons, the codename Quantum must be supplanted. Accordingly, this task is presently known as Neutron.

Present-day distributed computing platforms, for example, OpenStack, depend on a strategy for network administration known as programming characterized systems administration, or SDN. Conventional network organization depends intensely on the overseer to physically arrange and keep up physical system equipment and availability. SDN, then again, permits network executives to oversee system administrations in a dynamic and computerized way. Programming characterized organizing, and the product characterized server farm all in all, are regularly viewed as a fundamental establishment for versatile and proficient distributed computing. OpenStack Networking utilizes an administration called neutron-server to uncover an application programmable interface, or API, to clients and to pass solicitations to the designed network modules for extra handling. Clients can characterize network availability in the cloud, and cloud services are permitted to influence distinctive networks administration innovations to upgrade and power the cloud.

In the same way as other OpenStack services, Networking obliges access to a database for relentless storage of the network arrangement. In this part, you will be acquainted with the distinctive segments and components of OpenStack Networking, codenamed Neutron, and also different strategies in which Neutron can be conveyed and arranged from both programming and equipment points of view.

With SDN, we can depict complex systems in a safe multi-inhabitant environment that conquers the issues regularly connected with the Flat and VLAN OpenStack networks. For Flat networks, as the name portrays, every one of the inhabitants live inside the same IP subnet paying little mind to tenure. VLAN networking conquers this by isolating the occupant IP ranges with a VLAN ID; however VLANs are constrained to 4096 IDs, which is an issue for bigger setups, and the client is still restricted to a solitary IP range inside their inhabitant to run their applications. With both these modes, extreme division of services is accomplished through compelling Security Group rules. SDN in OpenStack is likewise a pluggable engineering, which implies we can module and control different switches, firewalls, and load balancers and accomplish different capacities in Firewall as a Service—all characterized in programming to give you the fine-grained control over your complete cloud base platform.

VLAN Manager is the default in OpenStack and takes into account a multi-inhabitant environment where each of those different occupants is doled out an IP address reach and VLAN tag that guarantees venture partition. In Flat systems administration mode, segregation between occupants is done at the Security Group level.

© Uchit Vyas 2016

U. Vyas, *Applied OpenStack Design Patterns*, DOI 10.1007/978-1-4842-2454-0_6

6.1 Routing

OpenStack Networking gives directing and NAT abilities using IP forwarding, iptables, and namespaces. A network namespace is comparable to chroot for the network stack. Inside a network namespace, you can discover sockets, bound ports, and interfaces that were made in the namespace. Every namespace has its own routing table and iptables process that give sifting and NAT. Namespaces are practically identical to VRFs in Cisco, routing occasions in Juniper JunOS, or route areas in F5 BIG-IP. With namespaces, there is no worry of covering subnets between networks made by occupants. Arranging a switch inside Neutron empowers occurrences to collaborate and speak with outside systems.

6.1.1 Physical Server Threads

The quantity of interfaces required per node is reliant on the kind of cloud being assembled and the security and execution necessities of the association.

A solitary interface for every server that outcomes in a joined control and information plane is all that is required for a completely utilitarian OpenStack cloud. Numerous associations convey their cloud thusly, particularly when port density is at a premium or nature is basically utilized for testing. Underway clouds, in any case, separate control, and information interfaces are prescribed.

6.1.1.1 Solitary Interface

For hosts utilizing a solitary interface, all activity to and from nodes and in addition inside OpenStack, SSH administration, and Programming interface movement crosses the same interface. This arrangement can bring about extreme execution corruption, as a visitor can make a disavowal of administration assault against its host by devouring the aggregate accessible transmission capacity. Not suggested for creation situations, this sort of setup should just be utilized for testing or POC.

The accompanying figure (Figure 6-1) shows the utilization of a solitary physical interface for all activity utilizing the Open vSwitch module. A physical interface lives in the system interface and handles outer, visitor, administration, and Programming interface administration activity.

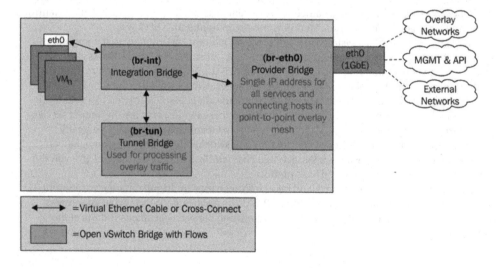

Figure 6-1. *Solitary interface*

In this figure, all OpenStack services and administration movement crosses the same physical interface as visitor activity.

6.1.1.2   Different Interfaces

To diminish the probability of visitor network transfer speed utilization influencing administration of movement and to keep up a legitimate security stance, isolation of activity between numerous physical interfaces is suggested. At least two interfaces ought to be utilized: one that serves as the administration and Programming interface and another that serves as the outer and visitor interface. On the off chance that this is required, extra interfaces can be utilized to further isolate activity. Figure 6-2 shows the utilization of two physical interfaces utilizing the Open vSwitch module.

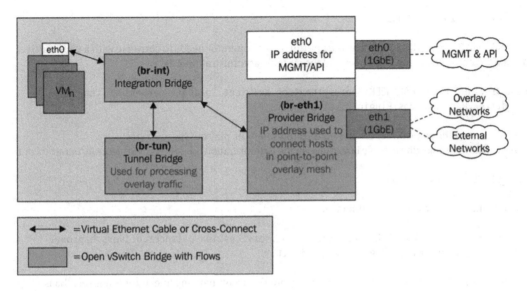

Figure 6-2. *Different interfaces*

In this figure, a devoted physical interface handles all activity coordinated to and from occurrences or other OpenStack networking administrations, for example, LBaaS and FWaaS, while another interface handles OpenStack Programming interface and administration movement.

6.1.2   Bonding

NIC holding offers clients the capacity to increase accessible data transmission by collecting links. Two or more physical interfaces can be joined to make a solitary virtual interface, or bond, which can then be set in the bridge. The physical switching foundation, in any case, must be fit for supporting this kind of bond. Notwithstanding conglomerating joins, holding can likewise allude to the capacity to make repetitive connections in an active/passive way. Both connections are all the while cabled to a switch or match of switches, yet one and only interface is active at any given time. Both sorts of bonds can be made inside CentOS or Ubuntu when the proper bit module is introduced. In lieu of inherent bonding procedures, bonding can be designed in Open vSwitch if desired.

6.2 Load Balancing

Load-Balancing-as-a-Service, otherwise called LBaaS, gives clients the capacity to circulate customer demands over numerous occurrences or servers. Havana is furnished with a module for LBaaS that uses HAProxy as the load balancer. Let's see how to coordinate LBaaS in our private cloud by following these directions:

We begin by introducing haproxy on the cloud controller hub utilizing the accompanying cli argument:

```
# yum install haproxy -y
```

Check if the load adjusting module is recorded in the administration modules in /etc/neutron/neutron. conf.

```
service_plugins=router,lbaas
```

To make HAProxy work legitimately, the neutron LBaaS operator needs to converse with a gadget driver as an interface between the load balancer and the systems administration API.

```
service_provider = LOADBALANCER:Haproxy:neutron.services.loadbalancer.drivers.haproxy.
plugin_driver.HaproxyOnHostPluginDriver:default
```

Finally, restart the Neutron server and on the compute hub, play out these strides:
Check if the load adjusting module is recorded in the administration modules in /etc/neutron/neutron.conf.

```
service_plugins=router,lbaas
```

So as to make HAProxy work legitimately,

```
service_provider = LOADBALANCER:Haproxy:neutron.services.loadbalancer.drivers.haproxy.
plugin_driver.HaproxyOnHostPluginDriver:default
```

Empower the Open vSwitch driver by remarking out the accompanying line in /etc/neutron/lbaas_ agent.ini record.

```
interface_driver = neutron.agent.linux.interface.OVSInterfaceDriver
[haproxy]
user_group = haproxy
```

Issue the accompanying orders to begin the neutron LBaaS agent:

```
# service neutron-plugin-openvswitch-agent restart
# service neutron-lbaas-agent start
```

We should imagine our load balancer administration tab in the dashboard by changing the accompanying settings in the /etc/openstack-dashboard/local_settings record:

```
OPENSTACK_NEUTRON_NETWORK = {'enable_ lb': True,
```

Restart the web server daemon in the cloud controller hub:

```
# service httpd restart
```

Here we go; our load balancer administration is prepared to be utilized from horizon. See Figure 6-3.

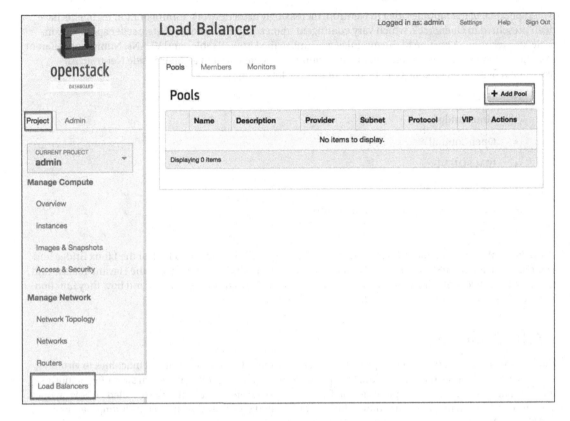

Figure 6-3. *OpenStack LB*

In addition, Neutron offers an arrangement of charges to completely oversee pools, individuals, virtual IPs, and health dashboards. The making of a load balancer and making it practical is direct and pretty simple so I am not going to cover that here.

6.3　Firewall

Security bunch usefulness was initially found in nova-network in OpenStack Compute and has subsequently moved to OpenStack Networking. This is a technique for securing activity to and from occurrences using iptables on the compute hub. With the presentation of Firewall-as-a-Service, otherwise called FWaaS, security is taken care of at the router instead of at the compute hub.

6.4　VPN

A VPN augments a private system over an open system, for example, the Internet. A VPN empowers a PC to send and get information crosswise over open systems as though it were straightforwardly associated with the private system. Neutron gives an arrangement of APIs to permit occupants to make IPSec-based VPN passages to remote entryways. In the Havana arrival of OpenStack, VPNaaS is a test augmentation with no ensured in reverse similarity in future releases.

6.5 Neutron Pluggable Modules

By temperance of the modules idea in Neutron, increasingly extra network administration highlights have been presented in OpenStack, which vary contingent upon equipment prerequisites, seller specs lock-in, scale, or execution. A portion of the modules may utilize the Linux IP tables and VLANs. Numerous different modules are made by outsider merchants that connect with their system gadgets inside Neutron. An assortment of neutron modules can be recorded as the following:

- Open vSwitch
- Linux Bridge
- OpenContrail
- IBM SDN VE
- Big Switch Controller
- Nicira Network Virtualization Platform
- Cisco Nexus 1000v

Among the specified modules for Neutron, in this segment, we will take a look at the Linux Bridge and Open vSwitch for OpenStack Neutron. Both modules are all around bolstered since the Havana release and give a layer for two switching bases. Now that you are most likely on edge to understand how they function independently, we should plunge into them.

6.5.1 Switching

Virtual switches are characterized as programming applications that interface virtual machines to virtual systems at layer 2, or the data layer of the OSI model. Neutron bolsters different virtual switching platforms, incorporating working in Linux spanning and Open vSwitch. Open vSwitch, otherwise called OVS, is an open source virtual switch that backs standard administration interfaces and conventions, including NetFlow, SPAN, RSPAN, LACP, and 802.1q; however a large number of these components are not presented to the client through the OpenStack API. Notwithstanding VLAN labeling, clients can assemble overlay networks in programming utilizing L2-as a part of L3 tunneling conventions, for example, GRE or VXLAN. Open vSwitch can be utilized to encourage correspondence among examples and gadgets outside the control of OpenStack, which incorporate equipment switches, system firewalls, storage gadgets, dedicated servers, and then some.

Accordingly, you should comprehend the two primary ideas:

Virtual system interfacing: At case boot time, another virtual network interface is made on the compute instance (running the hypervisor KVM as a matter of course), which is alluded as a tap interface. The previous interface is really the capable gateway that uncovered the virtual node to the physical system.

Virtual network bridging over: Let's handle this idea as straightforward thought. An extension permits two or more layer 2 networks to make a solitary network called total. How about we virtualize it: A Linux Bridge is a virtual extension associating numerous virtual or physical systems' interfaces.

6.5.1.1 The Open vSwitch

Normally, Open vSwitch is a virtual switch that encapsulates the developing idea of Software Defined Networking (SDN). In general, the previous idea plans to regard systems as projects that can be effectively conveyed and provisioned.

Additionally, what makes it the feline's whimper is the capacity to coordinate a virtual switching environment inside a physical one because of numerous upheld highlights. We should perceive how Open vSwitch is architected by looking at Figure 6-4.

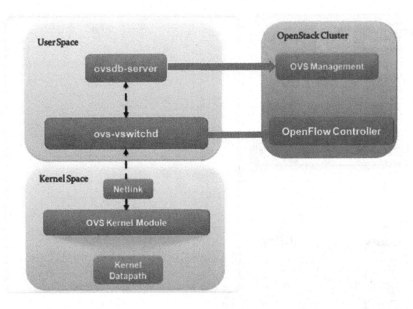

Figure 6-4. *Open vSwitch*

The general engineering should be direct:

- ovs-vswitchd: This is basically a project running inside the Linux bit model in every instance, which forces how the stream would be exchanged or sent.

- ovsdb-server: An Open vSwitch database is made in every instance running ovs daemon to keep up the virtual switch setup.

- OVS Kernel module: This is an information way where all bundles are sent and tunneled or exemplified and decapsulated.

Like the Linux Bridge module, Open vSwitch depends on the extension and its kernel modules. What has the effect are the extraordinary virtual gadgets that are made in the compute, have once you begin utilizing the OVS module. OVS utilizes more than one bridge; everyone will have a port with the same name as the extension itself as a bridge, of course.

6.5.2   Bridging

Keeping in mind the end goal to forward activity among nodes and to the virtual switch framework, there is dependably a need to make a scaffold, talked about already – and in addition, Linux 802.1q part modules to guarantee association with alternate networks. In the long run, the Linux Bridge module execution will include the use of no less than three virtual and physical gadgets, as portrayed in the Figure 6-5.

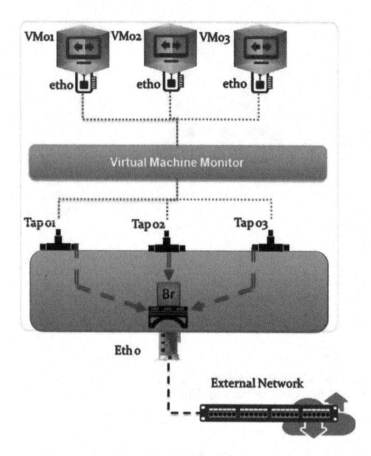

Figure 6-5. *Bridging in OpenStack Network*

A Linux Bridge Br-eth0 that holds a solitary physical eth0 interface and three virtual interfaces: Tap01, Tap02, and Tap03 relating to a system interface inside its individual visitor case. Movement from eth0 on a case can be seen on the separate tap interfaces and in addition the bridge and the physical interface.

Really, the past outline accepts a straightforward flat system in which no VLAN labeling may exist. The Ethernet outline trip where all tap interfaces lie in the same layer 2 communicate spaces is entirely straightforward. On the compute hub running the system agent, we can check how the bridge looks.

On account of a more muddled network setup where VLANs exist, the Ethernet frame trip turns out to be longer with one extra jump. Along these lines, before achieving the physical interface of the hypervisor having going through a virtual VLAN interface ethX.ZZ to tag and untag movement, it will require the accompanying composition as shown in Figure 6-6.

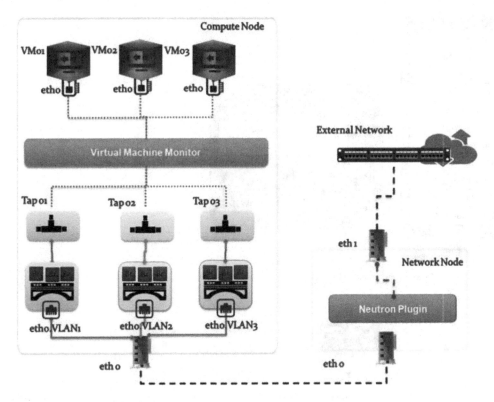

Figure 6-6. *Complex bridging*

Like other OpenStack segments, cloud administrators can part OpenStack Networking segments over numerous instances. Mini setup and deployments may utilize a solitary instance to host all segments, including organizing, compute, database, and messaging, while others may discover advantages in utilizing a devoted network instance to handle visitor movement directed through programming switches and to offload Neutron DHCP and metadata services. The accompanying graphs mirror a couple of regular segments arrangement models.

6.5.2.1   A Solitary Controller with One or More Compute Instances

In a situation comprising of a solitary controller and one or more compute instances, the controller will probably handle all network administrations and other OpenStack segments, while the compute instances entirely give compute assets.

The accompanying Figure 6-7 exhibits a controller instance facilitating all OpenStack administration and networking administrations where the layer 3 agent is not used. Two physical interfaces are utilized to give singular control and information planes.

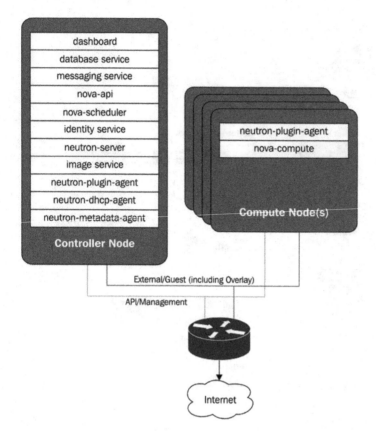

Figure 6-7. Solitary controller

This outline mirrors the utilization of a solitary controller and one or more compute instances where Neutron gives just layer 2 peers to nodes. An outer router is expected to handle directing between network portions.

The accompanying outline shows a controller instance facilitating all OpenStack administration and network administrations, including the Neutron L3 agent. Two physical interfaces are utilized to give separate control and information planes.

Figure 6-7 reflects the utilization of a solitary controller hub and one or more compute hubs in a network design that uses the Neutron L3 operator. Programming routing made with Neutron live on the controller hub and handle directing between associated inhabitant systems.

6.5.2.2 A Solitary Controller in Addition to Network Hub with One or More Compute Hubs

A network instance is one that is devoted to taking care of most or all OpenStack networking administrations, including the L3 operator, DHCP agent, metadata agent, and that's only the tip of the iceberg. The utilization of a committed network instance gives extra security and strength, as the controller instance will be in less danger of network and asset immersion.

The accompanying figure (Figure 6-8) exhibits a network instance facilitating all OpenStack networking administrations, including the Neutron L3 agent. The Neutron Programming interface, be that as it may, is introduced on the controller instance. Two physical interfaces are utilized to give separate control and information planes.

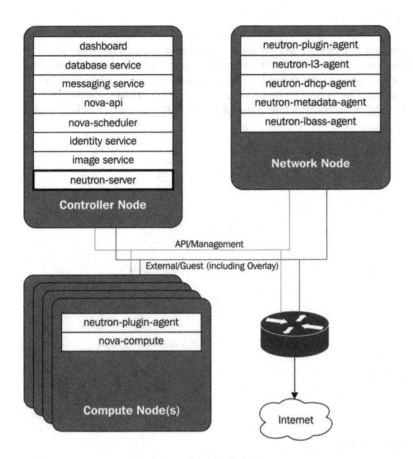

Figure 6-8. Solitary controller with multiple hubs

This chart mirrors the utilization of a committed network instance in a network setup that uses the Neutron L3 agent. Programming routers made with Neutron live on the network compute and handle directing between associated occupant networks. The Programming interface service and neutron-server and stay on the controller instance.

6.6 OpenStack Stack

As you may have speculated from the stack wording, this incorporates any gathering of associated OpenStack assets, including assets, volumes, virtual routers, firewalls, load balancers etc., that shape a stack. In any case, in what manner can stacks be made and overseen? Beginning from the Grizzly release, another coordination administration named heat has been included. Utilizing YAML-based layout dialects called Heat Orchestration Template (HOT), you will have the capacity to turn up numerous occasions, intelligent systems, and numerous other cloud administrations in a robotized style.

6.6.1   HOT Clarified

We should reformulate HOT more simply: characterize a legitimate format, and you get a running stack. On the off chance that you need to have a stack dispatch three examples associated by a private system and make it load adjusted, then the heat engine will expect the definitions for three occasions in your format, a network, a subnet, a load balancer, and three system ports. As depicted already, HOT has a particular structure taking into account the YAML sentence structure. A run-of-the-mill HOT structure would resemble the accompanying code:

```
heat_template_version:
description:
parameters:
  param1
    type:
    label:
    description:
    default:
  param2:
    ....
resources:
 resource_name:
    type: OS::*::*
    properties:
      prop1: { get_param: param1}
      prop2: { get_param: param2}
      .......
outputs:
  output1:
    description:
    value: { get_attr: resource_name,attr] }
              ......
```

OpenStack Networking offers the capacity to influence the distinctive innovations found in a server farm in a virtualized and programmable way. On the off chance that the inherent components are insufficient, the module design of OpenStack network administration takes into consideration extra usefulness to be given by outsiders, whether it be a business element or the open source group. The security prerequisites of the undertaking building the cloud, and the utilization instances of the cloud, will at last manage the physical design and detachment of administrations over the base instances.

This section secured a couple of points on Neutron modules in OpenStack. Open vSwitch and Linux Bridge have ended up being adaptable and an extraordinary answer for overseeing systems for nodes in the OpenStack private cloud. You should comprehend that Open vSwitch has had huge impact in this section because of its numerous elements when contrasted with the Linux bridge module. You likewise found out about the contrast among them and how you can control activity entrance and departure in your VMs environment by method for flow rules.

It was a decent chance to manufacture a first LBaaS setup by method for an appearance coordination administration manually and also using a glimpse of heat. You may understand the measured quality of such an arrangement engine and envision how you can construct a bigger stack in a matter of seconds. In spite of the fact that this section presented LBaaS, which may be extraordinary to scale cases for inhabitants, and despite everything you have to screen them and explore how to acquire a more straightforward answer for them, watch your OpenStack private cloud execution.

CHAPTER 7

■ ■ ■

Classifying OpenStack Storage

Storage is a noteworthy part of the bigger OpenStack platform, and between the distinctive storage sorts and seller-bolstered offerings, it can be a great deal to take in. OpenStack Object Storage and OpenStack Block Storage - regularly alluded to as Swift and Cinder, individually - are intended to work with different services of the open source OpenStack distributed computing and administration platform.

With regard to OpenStack, picking the right storage for your cloud can be the hardest piece of working out your surroundings. Each capacity seller has its own benefits. Some exceed expectations specifically utilizing cases, yet perhaps those utilization cases don't coordinate your purposes behind sending an OpenStack cloud. Perhaps you officially own some impeccably great storage and essentially need to repurpose your existing speculation. Whatever your circumstance, picking the right storage so that you get the execution, scale, and unwavering quality you need can be challenging.

Which storage innovation will fit into your OpenStack cloud usage? To answer this question, it is important to separate between various storage sorts, which will understand every utilization example of your subsequent choices. The way that OpenStack clouds can work paired with numerous other open source storage arrangements may be favorable position; however, it can also overpower.

7.1   Persistent vs. Nonpersistent

Truly, object storage versus block storage for OpenStack doesn't need to be a decision. Compositionally, block and object storage are integral answers for server farm outline. Accordingly, you are entrusted before all else as you need to choose what you require — persistent or ephemeral capacity?

7.1.1   Ephemeral Capacity

For straightforwardness, we will begin with the nonpersistent storage, which is also called transient storage or ephemeral storage. As its name proposes, a client who effectively utilizes a VM as a part of the OpenStack environment will lose the related disks once the VM is ended or by other means terminated.

7.1.2   Persistent Capacity

Persistent capacity implies that the capacity asset is constantly accessible. Fueling off the VM does not influence the information. We can partition it into two steady storage choices in OpenStack object and block storage with the code names Swift and Cinder, individually. We talked in basic terms about Swift and Cinder in earlier chapters. How about we plunge into every capacity technique in OpenStack mindfully and perceive how the two unique ideas are utilized to dump diverse technologies?

© Uchit Vyas 2016
U. Vyas, *Applied OpenStack Design Patterns*, DOI 10.1007/978-1-4842-2454-0_7

7.1.3   It's Object, Not NAS/SAN

Object storage permits a client to store information as objects by utilizing the HTTP APIs. On the off chance that you contrast an object storage framework with conventional NAS or SAN, it may be asserted that object storage is greatly improved than what was previously mentioned. You can allude to an object as a document representation. Objects can be differentiated with the following statements:

- Objects are put away in a level and immeasurable namespace. Not at all like customary storage frameworks, they don't protect a particular structure or a specific progression.

- Getting to the object storage Gadgets by utilizing a Programming interface, for example, REST or SOAP is impossible by means of any convention, for example, BFS, SMB, or CIFS.

- Object storage is not appropriate for elite necessities or organized information that is much of the time changed, for example, databases.

7.2   Shift toward Swift

Swift was one of the primary OpenStack ventures. It was produced by NASA and Rackspace, and the previous contributed toward the task by building up the code of the block storage of the OpenStack platform system. A couple significant changes to the capacity occurred in a limited capacity to focus time.

First, the rise of web and portable applications in a general sense changed information utilization. The second significant change was presented in the Product Characterized Capacity, which empowers an expansive dispersed storage framework to be worked by essential item storage. This drastically diminishes the expense of conveying information into an application as the individual part is not solid.

7.2.1   Design Implementation

By depending on Swift for the sensible programming administration of information rather than some specific merchant equipment, you increase unfathomable adaptability and components identified with organization scaling that are remarkable to a capacity framework.

Swift is in a general sense another sort of capacity framework. It is a monotonic framework as opposed to a disseminated framework, which implies that it scales out and endures disappointments without bargaining the information accessibility. Swift does not endeavor to resemble other capacity frameworks; it doesn't copy their interfaces. Rather, it changes how the capacity works. The Swift design is extremely dispersed, which keeps any Single point of Disappointment. It is additionally intended to scale on a horizontal plane. The parts of Swift comprise the following:

- The Swift proxy server: This acknowledges the approaching solicitations by means of either the OpenStack Object Programming interface, or simply the crude HTTP. It acknowledges record transfers, alterations to metadata, or container creation. What's more, it likewise serves documents or container postings to the web program. The server may likewise depend alternatively on the cache, which is generally conveyed with memcached, which enhances execution.

- The account server: This deals with the record that is characterized with the object administration. It portrays the capacity zone that characterizes its own enlightening data (metadata) and the rundown of containers in the record.

- The container server: This deals with a mapping of containers in the account server. A compartment alludes to the client characterized capacity zone in an account server. It characterizes a rundown of put-away protests in the container. A container can be theoretically like an example directory in a conventional filesystem.

- The object server: This deals with a real object inside a container. The object storage characterizes where the real information and its metadata is put away. Note that each object should have a place with a container.

Likewise, there are various procedures that play out the housekeeping undertaking on the extensive information stores. The most vital of these are the replication administrations, which guarantee consistency and accessibility through the cluster. Other post-preparing forms incorporate auditors, updaters, and other reapers.

7.2.2   Start and Overlook

What makes Swift an astounding handler of objects in a capacity framework is the way it treats the blob information and gives access by means of the OpenStack Programming interface.

7.2.2.1   Ordering the Information

Seeking, recovering, and ordering the information in an Object Storage Device is done by means of the broad utilization of metadata. In spite of the fact that a run-of-the-mill NAS storage utilizes the metadata, you ought to consider the way that the metadata in object storage Gadget is put away with the item itself in key-esteem sets. What makes it really brilliant is that the object storage gadget continues labeling the item regardless of the fact that it is cut or lumped with its metadata for capacity productivity reasons.

7.2.2.2   A Rich Programming Interface Access

The intermediary Swift process is the main procedure that can convey outside a capacity cluster, and what it does is listen and address a particular HTTP.

On account of the HTTP Programming interface, we will have the capacity to get to the OSDs. Then again, Swift gives dialect to particular libraries and APIs in PHP, Java, Python, etc.

7.2.3   Physical Outline Contemplations

The sign of Swift utilization is that it obliges you to take care of your information sturdiness and accessibility. As a matter of course, a Swift group storage outline considers a copy of three.

Along these lines, once the information is composed on a replica, it is spread crosswise over two different copies, which builds the accessibility of your information on one hand. Then again, you will require more storage limit. What's more, alluding to the main legitimate configuration in Part 1, "Outlining OpenStack Cloud Design," we have committed a network for capacity.

That was by reason first for intelligent system outline association and furthermore to alleviate the heap on the system by committing a different storage handler. Envision a circumstance where one of the capacity hubs with 50 TB falls flat when you have to exchange this enormous blob of information remotely to perform the required three-copy outline. It can take a couple of hours; however, we require it instantly! In this manner, consider the data transfer capacity decisively between your capacity servers and intermediaries. This is a justifiable reason motivation to put the focus on the physical configuration and the way the information is sorted out in Swift.

In the main stage, we saw that the records, containers, and objects shape the term information in Swift, which will require physical capacity. In this stage, the capacity hub will be built first. Keep in mind that Swift plans to detach disappointments, which makes the bunch more extensive as far as gathering as indicated by the hubs. In this way, Swift characterizes another progressive system that helps you theorize the intelligent association of information from the physical one:

- Capacity nodes: The coherent association proceeds with the capacity deliberation from the district, which is the most abnormal amount; zones inside area until we discover the capacity servers, which characterize the zone. An arrangement of capacity hubs frames a bunch that runs the Swift procedures and stores a record, a container, the object information, and its related metadata. What makes Swift novel is an exceptional storage coordinator that is mindful and is potentially used to characterize how your arrangement of hubs would be gathered by criteria.

- Capacity criteria: Contingent upon how the zones are set inside the accessible districts, Swift permits us to redo the way you wish to circulate information over a solitary area or numerous locales on particular storage equipment or a characterized reproduction cluster.

- Capacity gadget: This is the littlest grain of the Swift reflection information order. The capacity gadget can be the inside capacity hub's gadget or associated by means of an outside pile of an accumulation of plates in a drive's fenced-in area.

Figure 7-1 shows the flow for Swift.

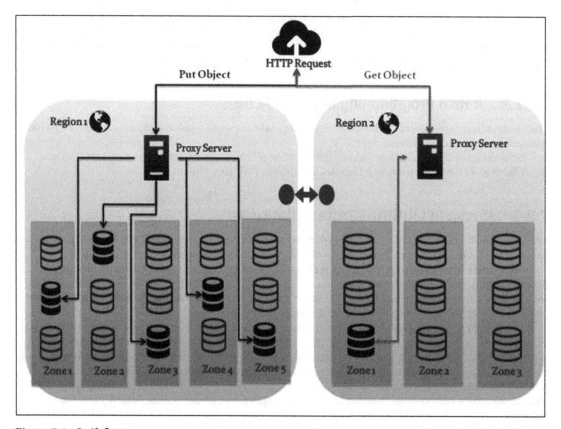

Figure 7-1. *Swift flow*

7.2.3.1 Where Is My Information?

Eventually, considering a MRC and searching for some example information over a group of capacity servers poses a question: how could Swift do that?

Whether the solicitation was to peruse or compose, the Swift servers need to outline information names to physical areas, which are called rings. Essentially, a ring is a group of tables that are disseminated to each hub in the bunch. Things being what they are, what is the reason that these tables exist all around? The answer is straightforward. This is on account of Swift reproducing information all around!

Does this not bode well? At the point when a procedure needs to discover some record-related information, it first begins looking in a nearby duplicate of the rings, which focuses to every one of the areas on the record ring for the information. For instance, the rings in Swift utilize the hash capacities to decide how to recover or store an object. At the point when utilizing a few drives as a part of a multiregion Swift environment, entangled hashing capacities can be utilized to fulfill such information areas.

Swift uses the ring-manufacturer application to make developer documents by record/container/object storage that contains data, for example, the reproduction checks, segment power, and the area of the capacity drives inside the group.

7.2.4 Swift Equipment

Essentially, we need to know what number of intermediary and capacity hubs (containers, records, and objects) we will require. Note that we can intelligently assemble containers, accounts, and/or objects in a hub to shape a capacity level. Note that the racks framed by an arrangement of capacity levels that are intelligently sharing a physical purpose of disappointment, for example, an association with a stand-alone switch, will be gathered into the same zone. How about we investigate a case of the configuration and deployment that we expect to have?

Let's say we need to deploy Swift having XFS as file System 50 TB of object storage from total of 3 TB storage with the cluster replica of 5 nodes along with 50 HDD for every chassis. With a couple of essential computations, we can finish up what number of capacity hubs we will require. Beginning with an essential point concerning the component or the XFS overhead gives an estimation of 0.5 percent, which gives an element of 1.0526. Then again, by accepting a group of five reproductions, the aggregate storage limit can be figured in the accompanying way:

```
50 * 5 imitations = 250 TB
```

Next, we will get the aggregate crude storage that is expected to compute the extent of the drive, as follows:

```
250 TB * 1.0526 = 263 TB
```

Presently, we have to decide the quantity of HDD that are required, as follows:

So let's say 263 divides by 3 where we get 86.7 so rounding the number gives us 87 drives. At last, the aggregate number of capacity hubs will be figured in the accompanying way:

```
87/30 = 2.9 => 3 nodes
```

We can utilize one intermediary hub for every three level hubs.

7.2.4.1 Where with What

Most likely, you will feel better with regard to picking the CPU or RAM limit in view of our past computations in Section 1, "Outlining OpenStack Cloud Design." What will be the situation in substantial conveyed storage frameworks?

We can go for the propelled CPU counts as we need to make our intermediary servers and capacity hubs a decent outfit for the item equipment that we plan to convey in the OpenStack storage framework. We won't spend a ton of cash while keeping up the base limit necessities. We should simply make it run.

The intermediary server in the Swift group will forward the customer's solicitation and send back the reactions over the capacity hubs, which may build the CPU usage.

Capacity instances will perform escalated disk I/O operations, while bearing more CPUs is exceedingly prescribed with respect to the Swift procedure handler for the replication and reviewing of information. Along these lines, with more drives per instance, more CPUs are required. How about we upgrade the methodology taking into account the CPU estimation in Part 1, "Outlining OpenStack Cloud Design." Thus, we as of now have 87 drives that are dispersed in three instances.

Expecting that we mean to utilize a CPU of 2 GHz processors with a proportion of cores to drives of 3:4, we can ascertain the quantity of cores that we will require, as follows:

```
(29 drives * 3/4 (core.GHz/drive))/2 GHz = 10.87 cores
```

As was asserted already, Swift suggests the utilization of the XFS filesystem, where it caches its instances in the RAM. More RAM suggests all the more reserving, and thus, a speedier object access. Then again, you may need to cache all instances in the RAM since you need to take mind that your system constraint does not prompt a bottleneck. We will begin with 2 GB RAM for each server.

At last, the most specific spec that comes now is the disks. Fundamentally, the intermediary instances won't require any extra drive, yet we have to discover a cost/execution fit for the capacity instances.

In the long run, the record and container servers can be sent with the utilization of SSDs, which will help the rate amid the confinement of the information. Then again, the object storage instances can be fulfilled by using the SATA/ATA circles with 6 TB plates, for instance. Note that the object storage instance is whining of a low IOPS. Consequently, you ought to include more disks until you get an adequate estimation of IOPS.

7.2.5 Networking with Swift

Our first system plan expects that an extra network is committed for the capacity framework. Indeed, we ought to remind ourselves that we are discussing a substantial base. All the more exact, Swift is turning into a major house with little rooms in our OpenStack platform arrangement. Be that as it may, Cinder can even now give a major room in a genuinely little house.

Hence, we will develop the Swift system by inferring more subnets, as follows:

The front-group system: Intermediary servers handle correspondence with the outer customers over this system. In addition, it advances the activity for the outside Programming interface access of the group.

The capacity cluster system: It permits correspondence between the capacity instances and intermediaries and between instance correspondence over a few racks in the same locale.

The replication system: We do think about the improvement of our framework size, correct? Along these lines, we will anticipate the same for the multiregion groups, where we commit a system fragment for replication-related correspondence between the capacity instances.

7.2.6   Pulling Swift to System

On the off chance that you didn't transfer the Swift cookbook, you can download it and add to your Chef cookbook from GitHub as per your openstack version and release:

    https://github.com/openstack/cookbook-openstack-object-stockpiling/tree/stable/havana.

Alternatively, we can allot, for every capacity instance, a triple Swift server: account, container, and object part while keeping devoted instances for the Swift intermediary server. A Swift node role can look like the following:

```
name "os-object-storage"
description "Swift Roles"
run_list(
  "role[os-base]",
  "role[os-object-storage-account]",
  "role[os-object-storage-container]",
  "role[os-object-storage-management]",
  "role[os-object-storage-object]"
  )
```

Even more, a Swift proxy role can look like the following:

```
name "os-object-storage-proxy"
description "Swift Proxy Role"
run_list(
  "role[os-base]",
  "recipe[openstack-object-storage::proxy-server]"
  )
```

For effortlessness, we can run the Swift intermediary server on the cloud controller. In particular, the Swift intermediary server ought to have admittance to the capacity system.

7.3   Shift toward Cinder

Since we are building the framework, we have to choose the best available storage. Without uncertainty, we have seen that Cinder is completely incorporated into OpenStack Compute, where clients can deal with their own particular storage needs by dealing with the volumes and the related depictions of these volumes.

It is basic to check the utilization instance of Cinder in our capacity outline. Like object and block storage is essentially a device for industrious storage. In the engine, volumes uncover a crude piece of capacity that can be connected to instances and which can store information for all time. Then again, Cinder oversees snapshots. Remember that the previous is a point-in-time duplicate of a volume, though you may have the capacity to make quick and transitory reinforcements by completely replicating a volume's information and putting away the same in the reinforcement framework. Be that as it may, the idea of the snapshot can be misconstrued when you depend on it only for long-haul reinforcement purposes.

In a general sense, block storage turns into a crucial prerequisite for virtual platform inside OpenStack that is agreeable to ephemeral capacity system. We ought to be happy that Cinder gives a block gadget that utilizations iSCSI, NFS, and Fiber Channel. Then again, we can even make it good with some other merchant back-end capacity availability. Additionally, Cinder helps you deal with the standards by restricting the inhabitant's use. You can restrain the amount utilization by aggregate storage used including snapshots, aggregate of volumes accessible, or aggregate number of depictions taken.

7.4 Picking the Right Storage

While managing the diverse storage frameworks inside OpenStack, you may ponder which outfit would be the best for your capacity arrangement. In light of our past dialogs, you should continue into the following stage and dispose of a couple of inquiries and situations to approve your decision.

Why should your surroundings bolster block storage and why not object storage platforms? Should you depend on the compute instances to store your diligent storage drives? On the other hand, will the outer instances be more helpful, mulling over your financial plan? Shouldn't something be said about execution? Do the inward clients require just dependable storage? Should they deliberately ignore its execution capacities? Do you require genuine excess storage to meet the necessities of information loss situations?

We will assume that block storage is prescribed for our OpenStack surroundings for the accompanying reasons:

- It gives persistent capacity to VMs, which ensures more consistency than Swift.

- It offers a superior read/write and input/output storage execution for the VM volumes.

- It determines the exchange off among execution and accessibility using outside storage when a capacity back end is upheld by Cinder.

- It has the snapshot facility to make new volumes for read/write utilization

All of a sudden, you may be enticed to believe that we should not utilize Swift; the response to this will be no! There are a few purposes for belligerence for Swift, some of which are the following:

- Swift is a solid match in the event that you wish to store substantial blobs of information, which incorporates an expansive number of images.

- It is appropriate for the going down of archival storage, which brings the base-related information in a sheltered zone.

- It is an exceptionally practical capacity arrangement that keeps the need to utilize an external RAID particular controller.

- With Swift, we can get to particular client information from anyplace; it can serve as a Google information web crawler.

7.4.1 Mixing Up the Storage as per Requirements

Once properly validated, the topology for any framework outline will experience an equipment arranging stage. For Swift, we will discuss object storage. How about we look at a case of equipment determination?

7.4.2 Can Cinder Give Us Something More...?

By depending on Swift to oversee object storage on common commodity hardware-based servers rather than particular merchant equipment, we pick up a great deal of adaptability requiring little to no effort. Nonetheless, when we touch base to invest some energy in our block storage, we confront a couple of different choices.

Block Storage varies from object storage with respect to the consistency. In a cloud domain, where machines rely on upon their volumes to run, it may be clear to treat this case in an unexpected way. In the event that you as of now have a unique merchant-based storage arrangement conveyed in your foundation, you can change the method for beginning starting with no outside help, which may be tedious, as well as costly. The magnificent thing about Cinder in OpenStack is that it underpins numerous capacity cluster suppliers. The previous uncovered block storage by method for Cinder drivers, for example, Dell, Hitachi, IBM, VMware, HP, NetApp, etc.

Cinder gives the accessible block storage driver support by the seller item. The capacities that are empowered by OpenStack release code names. Note that the vast majority of the suppliers give backing to conventions, for example, iSCSI in any case then Fiber Channel and NFS.

7.4.3   The Cinder Scenario

Dealing with the diverse storage pools from one unified administration interface makes Cinder send just the volume administration solicitations to your current storage framework. Now, you ought to acknowledge how OpenStack is interested in consistently incorporating the current pieces in your framework without you going through a nightmare when you wish to send what you precisely require.

Clearly, you may have a running OpenStack storage with one or various back ends where Cinder stands cheerfully. In any case, there are a few constraints that you should contemplate. As a framework originator, you may go over various handles that you may need to twiddle around with in a circulated storage environment. It begins when you move to the generation. A database director may all of a sudden find that VM has just about come to 96 percent at root partition. You don't have sufficient time to add another capacity cluster to the ESX server in the server farm, make another virtual disk, and append it through the vSphere.

This sort of circumstance gives an administrator lots of headaches: everyone hopes to hear things, for example, that it should work! Understand that virtualization can evacuate the cutoff points of hardware access for the endpoint machines, where the distributed computing worldview just uses it to give a hand and give precisely what you require without squandering assets. You should include another disk and your present case to develop a current home partition. For instance, generally making another /dev/sda5 essential partition and allocating it to your home segment by means of LVM will resolve the issue in almost no time. In a virtual situation, a precondition should be fulfilled to start with, which is the value that you need to pay to get profits by the cloud innovation. For instance, on the off chance that you expect to expand the virtual disk size from your vSphere while the machine is running, you should check whether it is thin provisioned. On the off chance that it is thick provisioned, you should reboot the machine in the wake of resizing the disk in the right segment. Thus, storage underway ought to be painstakingly taken care of and overseen by being aware of surprises that may occur.

Contingent upon the driver designed against OpenStack, you will be asked to check every methodology for what kind of restrictions you will confront amid the production stage. For instance, you won't have the capacity to extend a thick volume, which is connected with a snapshot. It is vital to know ahead of time what sort of volume you are utilizing as a part of request to stay away from an erroneous state. Then again, the matrix that was refered to before is extremely valuable to shoulder at the top of the priority list all the capacity administration functionalities. Some of them are not bolstered straightforwardly by Cinder, but rather you can utilize them from the local back-end asset storage administration.

7.5 Discovering Ceph

Take a glimpse at the framework mentioned beforehand, and you will discover Ceph! It is not only a driver that must be introduced and designed as a back end for Cinder. It is to a greater extent a standard open source dispersed capacity. Ceph can be utilized for object storage through its S3 Programming interface and also the Swift Programming interface. On the off chance that you plan to accumulate every one of the pieces from the object and system block devices, you ought to consider Ceph. Also, it is being created to uncover the filesystem interface, which is en route toward accepting backing from the environments like production. The idea of Ceph as an adaptable storage arrangement is just about the same as Swift that imitates information over the commodity storage instances. Do you believe that this is all there is? Obviously not. Ceph is a decent information consolidator that empowers you to snatch both the object and block storages in a solitary framework. You can even utilize it as a back end to look at images. In the event that it is concurred that Cinder is still prescribed in our block storage arrangement as we need its Programming interface, will you go for Ceph instead of Swift for the object storage back end? All things considered, this will be a troublesome question to answer in the event that you don't check how Ceph is more or less being architected. Figure 7-2 shows the engineering architecture of Ceph.

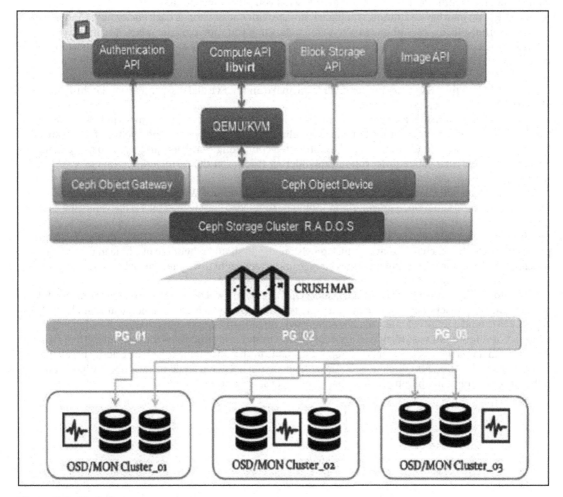

Figure 7-2. *Ceph flow*

The fundamental center of Ceph is the Reliable Autonomic Distributed Object Store (RADOS), which is in charge of the conveyance and replication of objects over the capacity group. As shown in the above figure, a block storage layer gives a RADOS block Device (RBD) for the object's back end. The astounding part in this engineering is that the RBD gadgets are meagerly provisioned inside the RADOS objects and because of the librbd library, objects can be gotten to by method for QEMU drivers, which make the supernatural connection amongst Ceph and OpenStack.

Ceph can be integrated seamlessly with OpenStack. It has emerged as a reliable and robust storage back end for OpenStack that defines a new way of provisioning the boot-from-volume instances. This new method of provisioning is named thin provisioning. Eventually, Ceph compromises on a nice concept, the copy-on-write cloning feature, allowing many VMs to start instantly from the templates. This shows a great improvement at the threading level along with an amazing I/O performance boost.

A large number of VMs can be made from a solitary master image gotten from a Glance image put away in a Ceph block device and booted by utilizing Cinder, which requires just the space required for their resulting changes.

We have been utilizing Cinder and its driver-empowered backing for Ceph. We as of now have a review of OSDs, which are the workhorses for object and block storage. In addition, segments can be made for the OSD hubs and doled out as various storage pools. Remember that this setup can be a case from numerous others. The basic point that you ought to stick to is the way you appropriate the Ceph parts over the OpenStack framework. In this illustration, we made the ceph-mon daemon keep running in the controller hub, which bodes well in the event that you mean to bring together all the administrations from a legitimate viewpoint. The ceph-osd hubs ought to keep running in the copy in independent storage hubs. The compute hubs need to know which Ceph hub will clone the images or store the volumes that require a Ceph client to keep running on them.

From the system point of view, the ceph-osd hubs will join the private storage subnetwork while keeping the hubs that are running the Ceph daemons in the administration system.

In this part, we secured an immense subject relating to storage in OpenStack. At this point, you ought to be more acquainted with the diverse storage sorts. We dug into an assortment of parts of Swift as a previous object storage answer for OpenStack.

Besides, you should now be happy with moving past the block storage segment for OpenStack. You will have the capacity to comprehend what fits better in your capacity outline against Cinder. We talked about the distinctive use cases for the OpenStack storage arrangements and grabbed a case from the numerous potential outcomes. You should now have the storage to think about a few variables, for example, filesystem, capacity convention, storage configuration, and execution.

At long last, the last segment of this part discussed how one can mix and send a block, object, and filesystem storage in a framework called Ceph. In this manner, because of its APIs, you can grab the extensive variety of chances that are given by OpenStack. Then again, settling on the right choice for your own particular storage arrangement is on you. Keep in mind that any storage use case will rely on upon your requirements or, at the end of the day, the necessities of your end clients.

CHAPTER 8

■ ■ ■

HA in OpenStack

HA may not be as basic as the name proposes: it's the push to kill any Single Purpose of Disappointment on each layer in your design. OpenStack segments can be gotten and appropriated to distinctive instances while keeping up a feeling of cooperation, which OpenStack is great at — once more, on account of our messaging administration. In this section, we will cover the following:

- See how HA and failover components can promise OpenStack business coherence

- Search for a workaround on the most proficient method to make distinctive OpenStack segments designed in HA

- Look at changed approaches to approve a complete HA setup

8.1   HA under the Extension

Every day, framework and system directors are confronted with another test by hitting the same point: we are meaning to make our foundation exceedingly accessible!

In the meantime, the IT chief adheres to his seat, drinking his coffee and cases: our IT framework works fine and our clients are fulfilled. Shockingly, you understand that telephone call from the help work area with a battling voice: well, the program said "page not found." Is the application server down? Clearly, the framework was not as profoundly accessible as it ought to have been. In spite of your additional time spent designing groups to be in uptime, as a general rule, servers won't not be reachable, and you then face a couple of uncommon instances, and you bring up this issue: why does it not fall flat over? To comprehend a HA foundation, on one hand, you should realize what HA offers to your surroundings and how.

Then again, you ought to remain nearby to test situations of coming up short over as exemplified in the accompanying genuine appear. Numerous framework overseers feel fortunate when they have purchased a capacity box that shouldn't come up short, and even has this composed: the arrangement that never yells I am disconnected. They guarantee that the new NAS box is exceedingly accessible. Unfortunately, this is never figured out. A power blackout happens and it removes the extravagant bunch from administration for a couple of hours with the goal that it can be restarted. On the off chance that you understood that you require an additional battery, then you can keep this physical occasion disappointment. Later, you overhaul its product bundle by tapping on Update the NAS. Sadly, the engineers of the NAS machine have incorporated another element in its HA bundle that makes the product unsteady, yet you are not ready to not make sense of that, as it is another release and no one had grumbled about it beforehand. Before long, a failover happens; however the server is inaccessible. It should have filled in as expected. In any case, futile, by checking in the racks, you made sense of that in the long run, the slave instance is turning into the master as per the sparkling LED light, which gets stuck while squinting! The failover is en route; however the framework is not responsive. There was a product bug in the last release. Now, the downtime increments again while the bug holds up to be altered. Unfortunately, you were the main NAS box customer to gripe about the new elements, which you may need to hold up to alter. This may take some time. A genuine since quite a while ago spontaneous disappointment could prompt a more serious issue!

© Uchit Vyas 2016

U. Vyas, *Applied OpenStack Design Patterns*, DOI 10.1007/978-1-4842-2454-0_8

The storage framework is not profoundly accessible any longer. Downtime is the careful adversary of HA. Inviting downtime can be arranged as you will just need to supplant a few bits of equipment. Then again, there are numerous explanations behind sudden downtime, for example, issues with equipment and programming, or any outer condition that prompts the disappointment of the framework. Regardless, we recollect that one of the few reasons for OpenStack clustering is to ensure that services stay running even during an instance disappointment. The HA usefulness intends to ensure that the diverse instances taking an interest in a given cluster work pair to fulfill certain downtime. HA, indeed, is a brilliant objective for any association where some valuable ideas can be utilized to achieve it with the least downtime like the following:

- Failover: Migrate an administration running on the fizzled instance to a working one (switch among essential and optional).

- Fallback: Once an essential is back after a fizzled occasion, the administration can be moved once again from the optional.

- Switchover: Manually change between instances to run the required administration.

On the opposite side, we may locate an alternate wording, which you may have in all likelihood effectively encountered, that is, load adjusting. In a vigorously stacked environment, load balancers are acquainted with redistributing a bundle of solicitations to less stacked instances. This can be like the superior clustering idea; however you ought to note that this cluster rationale deals with taking a shot at the same solicitation, though a load balancer intends to generally convey the task that its undertaking is handled in an ideal way.

8.1.1   HA Stages

It may be critical to comprehend the connection of HA configurations and setup in OpenStack. This makes it basic to recognize the distinctive stages of HA with a specific end goal to consider the accompanying in the cloud environment:

> S1: This incorporates physical instances, system and storage gadgets, and hypervisors

> S2: This incorporates OpenStack services, including compute, storage, and capacity controllers, and in addition databases and message queuing frameworks

> S3: This incorporates the VMs running on instances that are overseen by OpenStack administrations

> S4: This incorporates apps setup and running in the VMs themselves

The fundamental center of the supporting HA in OpenStack has been on S1 and S2, which are secured in this section. Then again, S3 HA has constrained backing in the OpenStack people group. By ideals of its multistorage back-end bolster, OpenStack can acquire occurrences that online the instance of host disappointment by method for live movement. Nova additionally underpins the Nova empty usage, which starts up API calls for VM clearing to an alternate host due to a compute instance disappointment. The fundamental center of the supporting HA in OpenStack has been on S1 and S2, which are secured in this section. Then again, S3 HA has constrained backing in the OpenStack people group. By virtue of its multistorage back-end bolster, OpenStack can acquire occurrences online the instance of host disappointment by method for live movement. Nova additionally underpins the Nova empty usage, which starts up API calls for VM clearing to an alternate host due to a compute instance disappointment.

Now, meeting these difficulties will drive you to procure aptitudes you never thought you could ace. Also, uncovering a base that acknowledges disappointments may recognize your surroundings as a private cloud. Keep in mind that this point is imperative in that all you have worked inside OpenStack segments must be accessible to your end client.

Accessibility implies that is an administration running, as well as presented and ready to be expended. How about we see a little review with respect to the most extreme downtime by taking a look at the accessibility rate or HA as X-nines. See Table 8-1.

Table 8-1. *Accessibility Matrix*

Nines	Accessibility %	Downtime per day
1	90	~ 2.4 hours
2	99	~ 14 minutes
3	99.9	~ 87 seconds
4	99.99	~ 8.7 seconds
5	99.999	~ 0.87 seconds
6	99.9999	~ 0.0087 seconds

Essentially, accessibility administration is a piece of IT best practices with regard to ensuring that IT administrations are running when required, which defines SLA:

- Minimized downtime and information misfortune

- Client fulfillment

- No rehash occurrences

- Administrations must be reliably open

A catch-22 may show up between the lines when we consider that wiping out the failure in a given OpenStack environment will incorporate the expansion of more equipment to assemble the cluster. Now, you may be presented to making more failure and, surprisingly more terrible, confounded foundation where support transforms into a troublesome assignment.

8.1.2   Mapping HA

What sort of measurements can be measured in an exceptionally accessible OpenStack framework?

HA methods seem to be expanding the accessibility of assets, yet at the same time, there are dependable reasons you may confront an interference sooner or later! You may see that the past table did not say any worth equivalent to 100 percent uptime.

To begin with, you may value the nonvendor lock-in trademark that OpenStack offers on this subject. Essentially, you ought to check the contrasts between HA functionalities that exist in a virtual base. A few HA arrangements give assurance to VMs when there is a sudden disappointment in the system. At that point, it will play out a reestablish circumstance for the occasion on an alternate node. Shouldn't something be said about the VM itself? Does it really work? In this way, we have seen diverse stages of HA. In OpenStack, we have as of now seen cloud controllers run reasonable administrations and compute, which can be any hypervisor segment itself!

Be that as it may, what ought to be contemplated, is the thing that truly influences the case remotely, for example:

- Capacity connection

- Fortified system gadgets

A decent practice is to outline the engineering with a methodology that is as straightforward as could be expected under the circumstances by monitoring each HA stage in OpenStack cluster.

A decent procedure to take after is to plan a conniving failure standard by decision. This catchphrase can be discovered anyplace in any framework. These days, huge IT bases are liable to experience the ill effects of database versatility over various instances. No matter what, the database in the OpenStack environment should scale also.

8.1.3 HA Terminologies

To facilitate the accompanying areas of this part, it may be important to recall a couple of words to legitimize high accessibility and failover choices later:

Stateless administration: This is the administration that does not require any record of the past solicitation. Fundamentally, every association solicitation will be taken care of taking into account the data that accompanies it. At the end of the day, there is no reliance between solicitations where information, for instance, does not require any replication. On the off chance that a solicitation comes up short, it can be performed on an alternate system.

Stateful administration: This is the administration where demand conditions become possibly the most important factor. Any solicitation will rely on upon the consequences of the past and the resulting ones. Stateful administrations are hard to oversee, and they should be synchronized with a specific end goal to protect consistency.

8.1.4 Deep-Dive with HA

Now, we can go further because of the developing distinctive topologies, and it is dependent upon you to choose what will fit best. The primary question that may come into your psyche: OpenStack does exclude local HA segments; how you can incorporate them?

8.1.4.1 Learning and Setting Up HA

HAProxy remains for High Availability Proxy. It is a free load adjusting programming apparatus that tends to intermediary and direct demands to the most accessible instances taking into account TCP/HTTP movement. This incorporates a load balancer highlight that can be a front-end server. Fundamentally, HAProxy characterizes two diverse load adjusting modes.

LB layer 4: Load adjusting is performed in the transport layer in the OSI model. All the client activity will be sent in view of a particular IP and port to the back-end servers. For instance, a load balancer may forward the inner OpenStack framework's solicitation to the Horizon web back-end gathering of back-end instances. To do this, whichever back-end Horizon is chosen ought to react to the solicitation under degree. This is valid on account of the considerable number of instances in the web back-end serving indistinguishable substance. The past case shows the association of the set servers to a solitary database. For our situation, all services will achieve the same database group.

LB layer 7: The application layer will be utilized for load adjusting. This is a decent approach to load parity network movement. Basically, this mode permits you to forward solicitations to various back-end servers in view of the substance of the solicitation itself.

Numerous load adjusting calculations are presented inside the HAProxy setup. This is the occupation of the calculation, which decides the server in the back end that ought to be chosen to procure the load.

You may consider how the past calculations figure out which servers in OpenStack should be chosen. In the end, the sign of HAProxy is a healthy check of the server's accessibility. HAProxy utilizes a well-being check via consequently crippling any back-end server that is not listening on a specific IP address and port.

8.1.4.2   Everything Can Fail But...

A VIP can be doled out to the active instances running all the OpenStack services that should be designed to utilize the location of the server. For instance, on account of a failover of the nova-programming interface administration in controller hub 1, the IP location will take after the nova-programming interface in controller hub 2, and every one of the customers' solicitations, which are the inner framework demands for our situation, will keep on working.

8.1.4.3   The Load Balancer Should Not Come up Short

The past use case accept that the load balancer never comes up short! Yet, in all actuality, this is a failure that we need to arm by including a VIP on top of the load balancer's group. Ordinarily, we require a stateless load balancer in OpenStack administrations. Therefore, we can attempt such difficulties utilizing programming like Keepalived.

Keepalived is a free programming apparatus that gives high accessibility and load adjusting offices taking into account its system so as to check a Linux Virtual Server (LVS) pool state. Keepalived utilizes the Virtual Router Redundancy Protocol (VRRP) convention to dispose of failure by making IPs exceedingly accessible. VRRP actualizes virtual directing between two or more servers in a static, default steered environment. Considering a master switch disappointment occasion; the reinforcement instance takes the expert state after a timeframe.

8.1.4.4   OpenStack HA in the Engine

Where it counts in the cloudy profundities of HA, the setup of our brilliant OpenStack environment is abundantly expanded! It might seem to be somewhat one-sided to support a given HA setup, however recollect that relying upon which programming clustering arrangement you feel more better about, you can execute your HA OpenStack setup.

Next, we will proceed onward to particular OpenStack center segments and wind up with uncovering diverse conceivable topologies.

8.1.4.4.1   HA in DB

Doubtlessly behind any group, there is a story! Making your database in the HA mode in an OpenStack situation is not debatable. We have set up MySQL in cloud controller instances that can likewise be introduced on isolated ones. In particular, keep it safe from water, as well as from flame. Numerous grouping systems have been proposed to make MySQL profoundly accessible. A portion of the MySQL structures can be recorded as follows:

Master/slave replication: A VIP that can be alternatively moved has been utilized. A downside of such a setup is the likelihood of information irregularity because of postponement in the VIP falling flat over. See Figure 8-1.

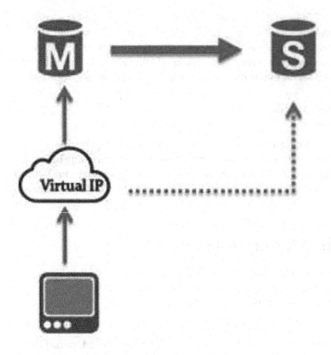

Figure 8-1. *Master/Slave replication*

MMM replication: By setting two instances, they both get to be masters by keeping one and only satisfactory composing inquiry at a given time. This is still not an exceptionally dependable answer for OpenStack database HA as in case of disappointment of the master, it may lose a specific number of exchanges. See Figure 8-2.

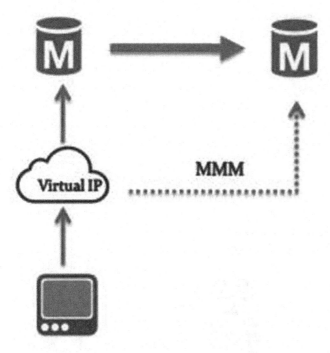

Figure 8-2. *Master/Master replication*

MySQL shared capacity: Both instances will rely on upon a repetitive shared storage. As appears in the accompanying image, Figure 8-3, a partition between nodes handling the information and the capacity gadgets is required. Note that a dynamic hub may exist any time. In the event that it comes up short, the other hub will assume control over the VIP subsequent to checking the latency of the fizzled hub and turn it off. The administration will be continued in an alternate hub by mounting the mutual storage inside the taken VIP.

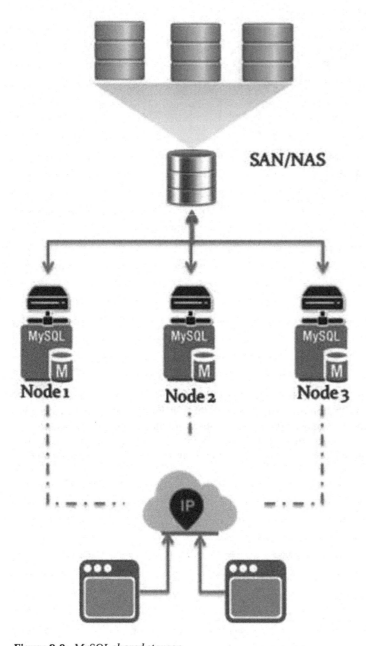

Figure 8-3. *MySQL shared storage*

Such an answer is magnificent regarding the uptime; however it might require an effective storage/ equipment framework that could be amazingly costly.

Block-based replication: One of the most received HA usages is the DRBD replication, which remains for Distributed Replicated Block Device. Basically, it reproduces information in the block gadget, which is the physical storage between OpenStack MySQL instances. See Figure 8-4.

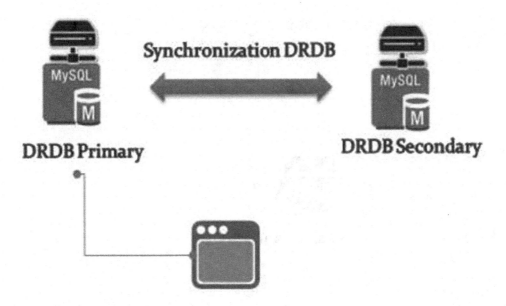

Figure 8-4. Block-based replication

What you require are just Linux instances. The DRBD takes a shot at their Linux kernel layer precisely at the base of the framework I/O stack.

DRBD can be a costless arrangement; however execution savvy, it can't be an arrangement when you depend on many instances. This can likewise influence the versatility of the replicated group.

MySQL Galera multimaster replication: Based on multimaster replication, the Galera arrangement has a couple of execution challenges inside an MMM design for the MySQL/innoDB database group. Basically, it utilizes synchronous replication where information is re-created over the entire group. When all is said and done, any MySQL replication setup can be easy to set up and make HA-skilled, yet information can be lost amid the coming up short over. Galera is firmly intended to determine such a contention in the multimaster database environment. An issue you may confront in a run-of-the-mill multimaster setup is that every one of the hubs attempt to upgrade the same database with various information, particularly when a synchronization issue happens amid the expert disappointment. This is the reason Galera utilizes Certification Based Replication (CBR).

Keep things straightforward; the fundamental thought of CBR is to accept that the database can move back uncommitted changes, and it is called value-based notwithstanding applying duplicated occasions in the same request over every one of the examples. Replication is genuinely parallel; every one has an ID check. What Galera can convey as an additional worth to our OpenStack MySQL HA is the simplicity of adaptability; there are a couple of more things to it, for example, joining a hub to Galera while it is robotized underway. The end outline carries a dynamic multimaster topology with less dormancy and exchange misfortune. See Figure 8-5.

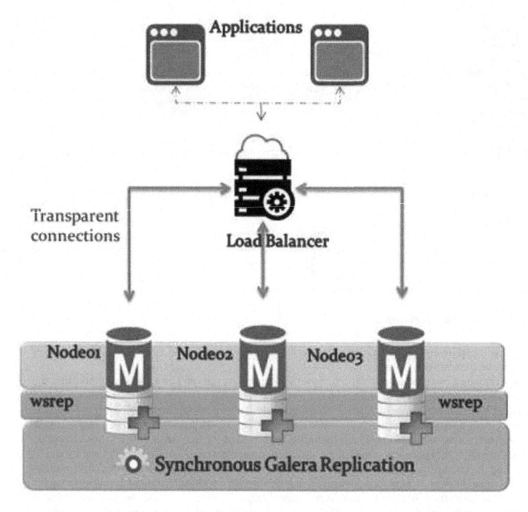

Figure 8-5. MySQL Galera multimaster replication

An exceptionally fascinating point in the last representation is that each MySQL instance in the OpenStack group should be fixed inside a Write-Set Replication (wsrep) programming interface. In the event that you as of now have a MySQL dual-master effectively working, you should introduce wsrep and arrange your cluster.

8.1.4.4.1.1   Don't get panic and utilize HA in DB

In this usage, we will require three separate MySQL instances and two HAProxy systems, so we can promise that our load balancer will come up short over in the event that one of them comes up short. Keepalived will be introduced in each HAProxy to control VIP. Distinctive instances in this setup will be doled out as the following:

```
VIP: 10.10.10.15
HAProxy01: 10.10.10.16
HAProxy02: 10.10.10.17
MySQL01: 10.10.10.18
```

```
MySQL02: 10.10.10.19
MySQL03: 10.10.10.20
```

With a specific end goal to execute HA on MySQL, play out the accompanying strides:

```
sudo yum install haproxy keepalived
```

modify your etc/haproxy/haproxy.cfg like following for both HAproxy systems:

```
log             127.0.0.1 local2
  chroot        /var/lib/haproxy
  pidfile       /var/run/haproxy.pid
  maxconn       1020    # See also: ulimit -n
  user          haproxy
  group         haproxy
  daemon
  stats socket /var/lib/haproxy/stats.sock mode 600 level admin
  stats timeout 2m
defaults
  mode    tcp
  log     global
  option  dontlognull
  option  redispatch
  retries                 3
  timeout queue           45s
  timeout connect         5s
  timeout client          1m
  timeout server          1m
  timeout check           10s
  maxconn                 1020
listen haproxy-monitoring *:80
  mode    tcp
  stats   enable
  stats   show-legends
  stats   refresh         5s
  stats   uri             /
  stats   realm           Haproxy\ Statistics
  stats   auth            monitor:packadmin
  stats   admin           if TRUE
frontend haproxy1     # modify on 2nd HAProxy system
  bind    *:3306
  default_backend         mysql-os-cluster
backend mysql-os-cluster
  balance roundrobin
  server  mysql01         10.10.10.18:3306 maxconn 151 check
  server  mysql02         10.10.10.19:3306 maxconn 151 check
  server  mysql03         10.10.10.20:3306 maxconn 151 check
```

Restart both HAproxy servers one by one. Presently, we will add the VRRP so in /etc/keepalived/ keepalived.conf. Be that as it may, initially, we go down the first arrangement file:

```
vrrp_script chk_haproxy {
  script    "killall -0 haproxy"
  interval 2
  weight   2
}
vrrp_instance MYSQL_VIP {
  interface       eth0
  virtual_router_id 120
  priority        111   # Second HAProxy will be 110
  advert_int      1
  virtual_ipaddress {
    10.10.10.15/32 dev eth0
  }
  track_script {
    chk_haproxy
  }
}
```
Once this configurations done, check it properly and set up Galera cluster using the latest stable Galera release, and then you are done here.

8.1.4.4.2   HA in RabbitMQ

RabbitMQ is for the most part in charge of correspondence between various OpenStack segments. The inquiry is genuinely basic: no queue, no OpenStack segment intercommunication. Since you get the point, another basic segment should be accessible and survive the disappointments. RabbitMQ is developed enough to bolster its own group setup without the need to go for Pacemaker or another clustering programming arrangement.

The stunning part about utilizing RabbitMQ is the diverse routes by which such an informing framework can achieve adaptability utilizing a dynamic/dynamic outline with the following:

RabbitMQ grouping: Any information or state required for the RabbitMQ intermediary to be operational is imitated over all instances.

RabbitMQ reflected queues: As the message queue can't make due in instances in which it lives, RabbitMQ can act in active/active HA message queues. Basically, queues will be reflected on different instances inside the same RabbitMQ group. Hence, any instance disappointment will naturally change to utilizing one of the queue mirrors.

Like any standard bunch setup, the first instance taking care of the queue can be considered as a master, while the reflected queues in various instances are absolutely slave duplicates. The disappointment of the master will bring about the choice of the most seasoned slave to be the new ace.

8.1.4.4.2.1   Don't panic and utilize HA in RabbitMQ

In this setup, we will utilize an instance to acquaint minor changes with our RabbitMQ occasions running in cloud controller instances. We will empower the reflected choice in our RabbitMQ dealers. In this case, we accept that the RabbitMQ segment is running on three OpenStack cloud controller instances, as follows:

```
VIP: 10.10.10.15
HAProxy01: 10.10.10.16
HAProxy02: 10.10.10.17
```

```
Cloud controller 01: 10.10.10.21
Cloud controller 02: 10.10.10.22
Cloud controller 03: 10.10.10.23
```

Stop RabbitMQ segment on the second and third cloud controllers. Duplicate the erlang cookie from the principal cloud controller and include the extra instances. Set the rabbitmq group and user with 400 consents in both the extra instances:

```
scp /var/lib/rabbitmq/.erlang.cookie\ root @cc02/@cc03 :/var/lib/rabbitmq/.erlang.cookie
sudo chown rabbitmq:rabbitmq\ /var/lib/rabbitmq/.erlang.cookie
sudo chmod 400 /var/lib/rabbitmq/.erlang.cookie
service rabbitmq-server start
```

On the cc02 node, run the following CLI arguments:

```
# rabbitmqctl stop_app
Stopping node 'rabbit@cc02' ...
...done.
# rabbitmqctl join-cluster rabbit@cc01
Clustering node 'rabbit@cc02' with 'rabbit@cc01' ...
...done.
# rabbitmqctl start_app
Starting node 'rabbit@cc02' ...
... done
```

On the cc03 node, run the following CLI arguments:

```
# rabbitmqctl stop_app
Stopping node 'rabbit@cc03' ...
...done.
# rabbitmqctl join-cluster rabbit@cc01
Clustering node 'rabbit@cc03' with 'rabbit@cc01' ...
...done.
# rabbitmqctl start_app
Starting node 'rabbit@cc03' ...
... done
```

Check the instances in the bunch by running them from any RabbitMQ instance:

```
# rabbitmqctl cluster_status
Cluster status of node 'rabbit@cc03' ...
[{nodes,[{disc,['rabbit@cc01','rabbit@cc02',
      'rabbit@cc03']}]},
 {running_nodes,['rabbit@cc01','rabbit@cc02',
                 'rabbit@cc03']},
 {partitions,[]}]
...done.
```

The accompanying order will match up every one of the queues over all cloud controller instances by setting a HA strategy:

```
# rabbitmqctl set_policy HA '^(?!amq\.).*' '{"ha-mode":"all", "ha-sync-mode":"automatic" }'
```

115

Alter its design record in each RabbitMQ bunch instance to join the group on restarting /etc/rabbitmq/ rabbitmq.config:

```
[{rabbit,
  [{cluster_nodes, {['rabbit@cc01', 'rabbit@cc02', 'rabbit@cc03'], ram}}]}]
```

We can continue to set up a load balancer for RabbitMQ. We have to just include another area in both the haproxy1 and haproxy2 instances and reload the setups:

```
listen rabbitmqcluster 10.10.10.15:5670
  mode tcp
  balance roundrobin
    server cc01 10.10.10.21:5672 check inter 5s rise 2 fall 3
    server cc02 10.10.10.22.101:5672 check inter 5s rise 2 fall 3
    server cc03 10.10.10.23:5672 check inter 5s rise 2 fall 3
```

Utilizing VIP to oversee both HAProxy hubs as an intermediary for RabbitMQ may oblige you to design each OpenStack administration to utilize the 10.10.10.15 location and the 5670 port. In this manner, you should reconfigure the RabbitMQ settings in every administration in the VIP, as follows:

```
# crudini --set  /etc/nova/nova.conf    DEFAULT rabbit_host 10.10.10.15
# crudini --set  /etc/nova/nova.conf    DEFAULT rabbit_port 5470
# crudini --set  /etc/glance/glance-api.conf   DEFAULT rabbit_host 10.10.10.15
# crudini --set  /etc/glance/glance-api.conf   DEFAULT rabbit_port 5470
# crudini --set  /etc/neutron/neutron.conf    DEFAULT rabbit_host 10.10.10.15
# crudini --set  /etc/neutron/neutron.conf    DEFAULT rabbit_port 5470
# crudini --set  /etc/cinder/cinder.conf   DEFAULT rabbit_host 10.10.10.15
# crudini --set  /etc/cinder/cinder.conf   DEFAULT rabbit_port 5470
```

8.1.4.4.3   Actualizing HA on OpenStack cloud controllers

Proceeding onward to the setting up of very accessible OpenStack cloud controllers requires a method for dealing with the segments running in the previous instances. Another option for the high-accessibility amusement is utilizing Pacemaker and Corosync. As a local HA and load adjusting stack answer for the Linux stage, Pacemaker relies on upon Corosync to keep up group correspondence in light of the informing layer. Corosync bolsters multicast as the default system arrangement specialized strategy. For a few situations that don't bolster multicast, Corosync can be arranged for unicast. In multicast systems, all the group instances are associated with the same physical system gadget, and it will be important to ensure that no less than one multicast location is arranged in the design record. Corosync can be considered as a message transport framework that permits OpenStack administrations running crosswise over various cloud controller instances to oversee the majority and group participation to Pacemaker. Be that as it may, how does Pacemaker cooperate with these administrations? Basically, Pacemaker utilizes Resource Agents (RAs) to uncover the interface for asset bunching. Keeping in mind the end goal to actualize HA on OpenStack cloud controllers and play out the accompanying strides:

```
# yum install pacemaker corosync
```

Corosync permits any server to join a bunch utilizing dynamic or active-passive issue tolerant design. You should pick an unused multicast address and a port. Make a reinforcement for the first Corosync arrangement file and alter /etc/corosync/corosync.conf as follows:

```
# cp /etc/corosync/corosync.conf /etc/corosync/corosync.conf.bak
# nano /etc/corosync/corosync.conf
Interface {
    ringnumber: 0
bindnetaddr: 10.10.10.0
mcastaddr: 52.225.10.10
mcastport: 4000
....}
Next generate SSH keys to setup proper communication channel start the services:
# service pacemaker start
# service corosync start
```

Set VIP for all nodes and proceed further on cloud controllers. We can set up a VIP that will be shared among the three instances.

```
# crm_mon -1
Online: [ cc01 cc02]
VIP    (ocf::heartbeat:IPaddr2):    Started cc01
```

So we can see VIP assigned to cc01. Set up RAs and arrange Pacemaker for Nova.

```
# crm configure primitive p_nova-api ocf:openstack:nova-api \
    params config="/etc/nova/nova.conf" op monitor interval="5s"\ timeout="5s"
# crm configure primitive p_cert ocf:openstack:nova-cert \
    params config="/etc/nova/nova.conf" op monitor interval="5s"\ timeout="5s"
# crm configure primitive p_consoleauth ocf:openstack: \
nova-consoleauth params config="/etc/nova/nova.conf" \
 op monitor interval="5s" timeout="5s"
# crm configure primitive p_scheduler ocf:openstack:nova-scheduler \
    params config="/etc/nova/nova.conf" op monitor interval="5s" \ timeout="5s"
# crm configure primitive p_ novnc ocf:openstack:nova-vnc \
    params config="/etc/nova/nova.conf" op monitor interval="5s" \ timeout="5s"
```

Same way you should be able setup RAs for Glance and Neutron.

In this part, you adapted the absolutely most vital ideas about high accessibility and failover. You additionally took in the diverse alternatives accessible to manufacture an excess OpenStack engineering with a hearty strength. You will know how to analyze your OpenStack outline by wiping out any failure over all segments. We highlighted distinctive open source arrangements out of the crate to arm our OpenStack foundation and make it as issue tolerant as could be expected under the circumstances. Diverse advancements were presented, for example, HAProxy; database replication, for example, Galera, Keepalived, Pacemaker, and Corosync. This finishes the initial segment of the book that covered diverse engineering levels and a few answers for winding up with an ideal OpenStack answer for a medium and extensive framework sending.

Index

© Uchit Vyas 2016
U. Vyas, *Applied OpenStack Design Patterns*, DOI 10.1007/978-1-4842-2454-0

Get the eBook for only $4.99!

Why limit yourself?

Now you can take the weightless companion with you wherever you go and access your content on your PC, phone, tablet, or reader.

Since you've purchased this print book, we are happy to offer you the eBook for just $4.99.

Convenient and fully searchable, the PDF version enables you to easily find and copy code—or perform examples by quickly toggling between instructions and applications.

To learn more, go to http://www.apress.com/us/shop/companion or contact support@apress.com.

Printed in the United States
By Bookmasters